THE
ENGLISH
summer
COOKBOOK

THE
ENGLISH
summer
COOKBOOK

thane prince

photographs by jean cazals

Bounty
Books

For my mother, who made me understand that you really can have more fun on the beach when it rains.

The English Summer Cookbook by Thane Prince

First published in Great Britain in 2005 by Mitchell Beazley, a division of Octopus Publishing Group. First published in paperback in 2008.

This edition published in 2011 by Bounty Books, a division of Octopus Publishing Group Endeavour House, 189 Shaftesbury Avenue, London WC2H 8JY
www.octopusbooks.co.uk

An Hachette UK Company
www.hachette.co.uk

ISBN 978-0-753721-95-7

A CIP catalogue record for this book is available from the British Library

Set in Scala and Gillsans

Colour reproduction by Sang Choy in China
Printed and bound by Toppan Printing Company in China

Commissioning Editor: Rebecca Spry
Executive Art Editor: Yasia Williams
Project Manager: Vanessa Kendell
Design and Art Direction: Miranda Harvey
Editor: Susan Fleming
Proofreader: Siobhan O'Connor
Photography: Jean Cazals
Stylist: Sue Rowlands
Production: Seyhan Essen
Index: John Noble

So many people to thank, for a book is never solely the author's work. Firstly and most deeply, my thanks go to Susan Fleming, who, from this book's conception to its final draft, has been so much more than just an editor and friend.

Thank you, too, to Sara Fox, my partner at the Aldeburgh Cookery School, along with the staff, Mel Brereton, Sharon Buzzard and Amy Landes, who make work a delight. Thanks, too, to all the many 'students' who have come time and again to listen to our jokes, laugh in the right places, cook so brilliantly and are gracious enough to praise what we do there.

Fantastic food suppliers in no particular order: Richard Emsden of Salter's Butchers', who is knowledgeable, skilled and open to ideas; Richard Ellis of 'Skipper's Choice', who finds me the freshest fish at almost a moment's notice; Dean Fryer, one of the remaining beach fishermen in Aldeburgh, who remains an enthusiastic exponent of his craft; Mark Windows of Cromer, who brings me the sweetest lobsters and crabs caught in the wild and unpredictable North Sea. Albert Webster merits special thanks both as my garden guru and for bringing me gifts of sweet peas, carrots and garlic – an endless list. Thanks, too, to his elegant wife, Margaret, for her forbearance and chauffeuring. In London Patricia Michelson, cheese goddess; Chris Godfrey, butcher; and Brindisa, purveyor of delicious oils, have all influenced my palate.

A huge thank you to Mitchell Beazley for publishing this book and so giving me a chance to write about a subject close to my heart: Becca Spry for commissioning it; Miranda Harvey for designing it and holding my hand while the photographs were taken; Jean Cazals for taking such lovely shots; and Sue Rowlands for adding her sense of style.

Friends and relatives tend to get taken for granted, so special thanks to Gill Ib for washing up and making me laugh, and to Diana Meller for her sustaining phone calls.

And finally thank you to Bob, Jade and Amber, who have seen me through seven books before this one, yet still managed to smile when I announced I was going to write another. Lucky the woman with a supportive and loving family.

contents

introduction

Is there anything more enigmatic than an English summer? Try explaining the concept to someone who doesn't live here, and they can't grasp it. But the weather is ghastly they will say – it's cold, it always rains, you can't plan anything. And to an extent they are right, but to focus simply on sunshine and precision planning would be to miss the whole point of an English summer, for reality has only a small part to play in one's enjoyment of it.

I love the rhythm of an English summer, the steady stream of events that mark the passing weeks: cake stalls at the village fête, picnics by the river, lunch at the races, cricket club teas, a beach barbecue followed by a midnight swim .... These tread through the summer like beads in a necklace, and each is made more delightful by delicious seasonal food.

Summer is a time when English gardens show their true magnificence, and nowhere is that more evident than in the vegetable garden, with even the smallest plot yielding fresh herbs and plump dew-kissed produce. Farmers' markets burgeon with fruits, vegetables, juices and jams, and pick-your-own farms open their gates to crowds of berry lovers.

English eating is quintessentially seasonal. From the first asparagus tip to the first plum, the English summer yields some of our most luscious and delicious foodstuffs. Dover sole, crabs and lobster are fished by local boats, hedgerows yield elderflowers for their heady cordial, and early walkers collect mushrooms for a country Sunday brunch.

Summer is a social time, for having spent winter in front of the hearth, we rush outside to embrace the easy camaraderie that fine weather brings. Sharing a picnic rug, borrowing a corkscrew, building a sandcastle or playing an impromptu game of beach cricket changes even the most reserved of us into social animals.

And then there is the sheer delight of a successful summer day. The pleasure to be had in dreaming of sun-filled picnics is all very fine, but the real joy comes in the laughter of drinking the champagne quickly so it won't be diluted by the downpour happening around you. And whilst walking along the tideline in the glow of a warm sunset is romantic, battling through a bracing headwind gives a greater sense of achievement to the venture.

Lest you think I love to suffer, I admit that sun-soaked wasp-free summers would be my preference. But I lived for a time in the United States and found the predictability of the weather made summer outings rather less of an adventure. No need to pack the brollies, flasks of hot soup or fleeces when picnicking in New Jersey. Delight there was, but no great sense of triumph. For it is only when against all the odds the weather is perfect, the company harmonious, the mood jolly and the picnic spot serene that the sense of special becomes apparent.

And English summers are indeed special – a time for good food, good wine, good company and good conversation. And, who knows, we might even need to use that umbrella as a parasol!

early
summer
lunch

The very beginning of summer offers such promise. Spring rain and longer, sunnier days have worked their yearly magic, the garden begins to look inviting, and meals under the walnut tree beckon. Whilst it's probably not quite warm enough to eat outside, a celebration lunch held in anticipation of good times to come is called for. Early summer offers us a wonderful chance to eat foods at their youngest and sweetest. Asparagus, broad beans and baby new potatoes speak eloquently of English summer food at its most delicious. Herbs picked now are at their greenest, freshest stage before the summer sun deepens both their colour and their perfume. Gooseberries make a fleeting appearance in the market, with luck appearing before the end of the elderflower season, and crab – my favourite crustacean – is perfectly matched with peppery salad leaves such as rocket and watercress.

early summer lunch

Bread is very easy to make, I promise. The yeast must be frothy before you add it to the flour, and the room needs to be comfortably warm. The rest is child's play. If you have no rye flour or oatmeal, simply replace these with extra white or wholemeal flour. Replace the sourdough 'mother' with buttermilk, natural yoghurt or soured cream. The bread will still stun your friends and taste delicious (it also freezes well).

seeded sourdough bread

1 teaspoon runny honey | 1 tablespoon dried yeast | 450g strong plain flour | 50g rye flour | 50g oatmeal | 2 teaspoons fine salt | 4 tablespoons olive oil | 4 tablespoons sourdough starter (optional, see page 158) | 30g each of sunflower seeds and pumpkin seeds | 45g raisins

makes 2 loaves

1 Mix the honey into 300ml warm water, then beat in the yeast. Leave in a warm place for 15 minutes.

2 In a large bowl combine the flours, oatmeal and salt. Add the by now frothy yeast mixture, oil and sourdough starter (if using), stirring everything together. Tip the dough on to a board and knead until smooth, about 6–7 minutes. The dough should be quite sticky, so don't add more flour. Pop it back into the bowl, cover with a dry cloth and leave in a warmish place to rise for about 1½ hours, or until doubled in size.

3 Turn the dough back out on to a board, add the seeds and raisins, and knead everything together well. Divide the dough into two pieces, shape each piece into an oblong loaf, and place on a floured baking sheet. Dust with a little extra flour for that boutique bakery look!

4 Again leave for about an hour until doubled in size. Meanwhile, preheat the oven to 200°C/400°F/Gas mark 6.

5 Bake the loaves for 25–30 minutes, or until the bread sounds hollow when the base is tapped. Cool on a rack.

Crab is at its best in very early summer or early autumn. During the long midsummer days, crabs are more intent on reproduction than on eating, and so crabs caught then may contain little meat. When buying an undressed crab, weigh it in your hand to check it feels about right. Crab must be eaten fresh and it really is best to dress it yourself.

I have suggested three fragrant herbs for the white meat part of the salad. Choose only one. I would probably go with the gently anise flavour of chervil if it had grown enough by now. Tarragon has a more robustly aniseed flavour, and coriander lends an air of the East to the dish.

This salad has two distinct parts, which may make it sound a bit fancy, but it really does let your carefully picked crab meat show to its full potential.

chilli crab salad

mixed baby salad leaves (this is the moment for all those tasty slightly bitter leaves such as rocket, mizuna, mustard and red beet leaves) | sea salt and black pepper | white and brown meat from 2 medium crabs, kept separate | grated zest and juice of 1 lime | 1 small chilli, seeded and chopped | 2 tablespoons chopped chervil, coriander or tarragon | extra virgin olive oil | 3 tablespoons mayonnaise | good shake of Tabasco sauce | 1 tablespoon wine vinegar | handful of parsley leaves, chopped

serves 6

1   Wash and dry the salad leaves. If they are very small I find it best to spread the leaves on a clean tea towel and allow them to dry that way rather than subjecting them to the rough treatment of a salad spinner. Place them in a large bowl and season with salt and pepper.

2   In another bowl mix the white crab meat with the lime zest, chilli and chosen herb. Toss the mixture and season with salt and pepper, then add the lime juice and olive oil to taste.

3   In yet another bowl mix the brown meat, mayonnaise, Tabasco and some salt and pepper.

4   Lay out your plates. Now dress the salad leaves with about 2 tablespoons oil and the wine vinegar. Toss and divide between the plates. Spoon on a portion of brown meat, then scatter over the white meat. Sprinkle with parsley and serve with seeded bread (see page 11).

Lamb, that staple of summer Sunday lunches, deepens in flavour as the year progresses. Early lamb, reared for Easter, has a light, gentle taste far removed from the muttony character lamb develops as it ages. This light-coloured meat continues into early summer and is much too delicate for heavy-handed cooking, so no spiking heavily with rosemary and garlic this time.

Ask your butcher for a shoulder or leg of young lamb. Shoulder of lamb is fattier than leg, but to my mind tastes sweeter – you choose.

I'm serving a light minted butter sauce with the lamb. This will also dress the vegetables and potatoes. Mint is the herb of choice here. Do look in garden centres for the many different varieties of mints available, and grow several of them.

roast early lamb

1 large onion, peeled and sliced | few sprigs of young rosemary | 1.75kg leg or shoulder of lamb | butter | sea salt and black pepper

serves 6

1 Preheat the oven to 200°C/400°F/Gas mark 6.

2 Lay the onion and rosemary in the base of a roasting pan. Generously smear the lamb with butter, season well and lay on the bed of onion and rosemary. Pour in about 150ml water and roast the lamb, basting every 20 minutes, for 1½ hours if you like your lamb pink, or 2 hours if you prefer it more well done. If you're roasting shoulder of lamb, turn the joint each time you baste.

3 Remove the lamb from the oven and allow it to sit in a warm place for at least 15 minutes before carving. (I would arrange to take the lamb out of the oven just as I sit down for my starter. It will then be perfectly rested when you come to carve it.)

4 Serve with minted hollandaise sauce alongside early summer vegetables and potatoes (see page 16).

Have everything ready – the wine reduced, the butter melted and ready to reheat, yolks whizzed in the processor – and make this sauce whilst the vegetables cook. It's foolproof and only takes about 3 minutes.

minted hollandaise sauce

100ml white wine | **1 shallot, peeled and finely chopped** | **140g butter** | **3 large egg yolks** | **sea salt and black pepper** | **Tabasco sauce** | **juice of 1 lemon** | **good handful of young mint leaves, picked from the stems**

serves 6

1 In a small pan boil the wine and shallot together until reduced by half. Melt the butter in a separate pan.

2 Place the egg yolks into a blender or processor, and season well with salt and pepper. Add a dash of Tabasco and a squeeze of lemon juice, and whizz to mix.

3 Now with the motor running pour in the hot wine mixture followed by the hot butter, adding this in a thin stream. Add the picked mint leaves and whizz for a further few minutes. Taste, correct the seasoning and serve.

early summer vegetable mix

Since having my own vegetable garden I have come to cooking my vegetables in the following fashion – born, I must say, of necessity. I found that when gathering my crop there were often too few of any single variety of beans, peas or courgettes to make a meal. I consequently started cooking whatever was young and fresh regardless of the mix, and it works wonderfully well.

Simply cut the vegetables to a uniform size and add them to a large shallow pan of boiling salted water in order of cooking time. So it's usually long beans first, then courgettes and finally spinach. Broad beans are best cooked without salt, as this toughens their skins, so these should always be cooked in a separate pan of unsalted boiling water.

This wonderfully fragrant cordial is simple to make and delicious in summer drinks, sorbets and jellies. Gather the flowers when at their most fragrant, a day or so after all the florets have opened and first thing in the morning. It's essential to use spotlessly clean utensils; this is to minimise the risk of the cordial fermenting. Store in a cool, dark place: an outdoor shed, cellar or garage is ideal.

elderflower cordial

1kg white caster sugar | **4 large lemons** | **8 limes** | **4 oranges** | **about 20 large elderflower heads** | **55g citric acid**

makes 2.5 litres concentrate

I Dissolve the sugar in 1.8 litres water and bring to the boil. Boil for 5 minutes.

2 Wash the citrus fruit in hot water, scrubbing with a scourer to remove any wax on the skins. Now chop them up into about 2.5cm cubes and place these, along with the flower heads, in a large, spotlessly clean glass or china bowl. Pour over the sugar syrup, stir in the citric acid and cover with a clean cloth. Leave the bowl in a cool, dark place for four days, stirring each day with a clean metal spoon.

3 Strain the syrup through scalded muslin into a large saucepan (not aluminium), and bring it just up to boiling point. Remove from the heat, allow to cool, then pour into sterilised bottles. I use screw-top mineral water bottles as these are clean and of a handy size.

One of my all-time favourites, gooseberry ice-cream has a wonderfully fresh flavour and delicate colour. An added joy of making this ice-cream is that you don't have to top and tail the gooseberries! Poach them, then rub through a sieve, which deals with skins and pips – so not needed in an ice-cream.

gooseberry ice-cream

900g fresh gooseberries, rinsed | **50ml elderflower cordial (see page 17)** | **icing sugar (optional)**
For the custard base **600ml single cream** | **6 large egg yolks** | **200g caster sugar**

serves 6

1 Start by making the custard. Heat the cream to boiling point. Meanwhile, whisk the egg yolks and sugar together until light and smooth. Pour on the hot cream and return the mixture to the pan. Cook over a low heat, stirring constantly, until the custard thickens. Do not allow the mixture to boil. Transfer to a bowl and cover the surface of the custard with clingfilm, extending it up the sides of the bowl – this is to prevent a skin forming. Leave to cool, then refrigerate until chilled.

2 Place the gooseberries in a large pan with 4 tablespoons water and bring to the boil. Cover and simmer until tender, about 5–7 minutes. Mash the gooseberries, then rub the purée through a sieve to remove the skin, pips etc. Chill.

3 Mix the chilled gooseberry purée, custard and elderflower cordial together well. Taste. If you find the mixture too sour you can add a little icing sugar, but remember the flavour of this ice is meant to be quite fresh and tangy.

4 Churn in an ice-cream machine according to the manufacturer's instructions. Alternatively, pour into a shallow tray and freeze in the coldest part of your freezer. Beat the ice-cream from time to time to break up any ice crystals. Remove from the freezer about 30 minutes or so before you need it, then serve with cardamom biscuits (see opposite).

Always use freshly ground spices. I keep an electric grinder dedicated to this purpose. It may sound a little fussy, but would you serve coffee that had been ground as long ago as the mixed spice in your kitchen cupboard? Anything that relies on volatile oils for flavour must be freshly ground.

crisp cardamom biscuits

110g butter, softened | **55g caster sugar** | **55g soft brown sugar** | **1 large egg** | **½ teaspoon vanilla extract** | **½ teaspoon baking powder** | **pinch of sea salt** | **½ teaspoon ground cinnamon** | **½ teaspoon ground cardamom** | **140g plain flour** | **55g cornmeal/polenta**

serves 6

1 Mix the butter and sugars together, add the egg, then all the remaining ingredients, stirring until you have a smooth dough. Chill for 30 minutes.

2 Roll out the dough between sheets of clingfilm or wax paper until 3mm thick. Remove the clingfilm, cut into shapes – whatever you like (I use a 7.5cm cutter, making about 20 biscuits) – and chill for 15 minutes. Meanwhile, preheat the oven to 350°F/180°C/Gas mark 4.

3 Bake the biscuits until lightly golden, about 12–20 minutes, depending on size.

cake stall

Is there anyone whose eyes don't light up when they see a cake stall? Cornerstone of the village fête, school fundraiser and Women's Institute market, cake stalls have long been a passion of mine. Home-made cakes speak of warm kitchens, soft butter beaten with gritty sugar, split vanilla pods and, possibly best of all, of bowls and spoons to lick. Cake stalls are wonderfully egalitarian, providing joy for each and every one of us. The first rule of successful cake stalls is to have sufficient cakes to supply demand. Secondly, always have a range of prices. Thirdly, do provide clean bags or boxes to carry the cakes home. Not everyone is like me and wants to eat them there and then! Always wrap cakes for stalls well, add a label including the full list of ingredients, and remember to charge a realistic price. These home-made cakes are special – don't mark them too low!

cake stall

I make this cake in a food processor, adding whole nuts and letting the action of the blade chop them roughly. To make by hand, simply chop the nuts first. Don't forget to label this cake well, as it contains nuts.

banana bread

190ml vegetable oil, plus extra for greasing | **3–4 medium ripe bananas, peeled and well mashed** | **3 medium eggs, beaten** | **1 teaspoon vanilla extract** | **125g wholemeal flour** | **125g plain flour** | **2 level teaspoons baking powder** | **½ teaspoon salt** | **115g light muscovado sugar** | **55g shelled pecans or walnuts, chopped**

makes 1 loaf

1 Grease a 900g loaf tin, and preheat the oven to 160°C/325°F/Gas mark 3.

2 Mix the mashed bananas, eggs, vanilla and vegetable oil together, beating until the mixture is well combined.

3 In a separate bowl mix the flours, baking powder, salt and sugar, breaking down any lumps the sugar may have. Now add this to the wet ingredients, and lastly add the chopped nuts.

4 Pour the mixture into the prepared loaf tin and bake in the preheated oven for 55–65 minutes – a skewer inserted in the centre of the cake should come out clean. Allow to cool for at least 30 minutes before removing from the tin.

As a child I lived in East Anglia, where American air force bases abounded and packets of Betty Crocker brownie mix were passed between locals and the service wives. Whilst probably not an English tradition they definitely formed part of my childhood, and I think fifty years is enough time to call these delicious bar cakes our own. The secret to perfect brownies is to remove them from the oven while the centre is still a little soft.

double chocolate mint brownies

225g butter, softened, plus extra for greasing | 200g plain flour | 55g cocoa powder | I teaspoon baking powder | ½ teaspoon salt | 285g caster sugar | I teaspoon vanilla extract | 4 medium eggs | 100g shelled walnuts, roughly chopped

For the icing 225g icing sugar | 55g butter, softened | peppermint essence, to taste | 170g good plain chocolate

makes 20–30 brownies

I Grease and line a 33 x 23 x 5cm roasting tin with non-stick paper, and preheat the oven to 180°C/350°F/Gas mark 4.

2 Sift the flour, cocoa, baking powder and salt together. In a large bowl, cream the butter and sugar together until light, then add the vanilla extract. Beat in the eggs, one at a time. Add a spoonful of the dry ingredients if the mixture starts to split and curdle. Now fold in the remaining flour mixture, along with the walnuts.

3 Pour the mixture into the roasting tin, and bake in the oven for 20–25 minutes. Remove from the oven and allow to cool completely in the tin.

4 Make the icing by beating the icing sugar, butter and I tablespoon hot water together until light and fluffy. If the mixture seems a little stiff, add a few more drops of water. Now add peppermint essence to taste. Spread this icing over the top of the cake, still in the tin, making the top as smooth as possible. Chill in the refrigerator for at least I hour.

5 Break the chocolate into pieces, and melt in a bowl over a pan of simmering water (the bowl must not touch the water). When the chocolate is runny, spread over the peppermint icing. Allow to set, then cut the brownie in the tin into small pieces.

Satsumas seem to be available year-round now, but a thin-skinned orange well scrubbed and with any pips removed would work as well.

orange pound cake

115g butter, softened, plus extra for greasing | 170g plain flour, plus extra for dusting | 2 teaspoons baking powder | 170g caster sugar | 3 large eggs | 1 seedless satsuma | finely grated zest of 1 lemon | 140ml soured cream

makes 1 cake

1 Grease and flour a 750g loaf tin and preheat the oven to 180°C/350°F/Gas mark 4.

2 Sift the flour and baking powder together. Cream the butter and sugar together until light and fluffy, then beat in the eggs, one at a time, adding a tablespoon of flour after each egg.

3 Meanwhile, place the satsuma, lemon zest and soured cream in a blender or processor, and whizz until smooth. Now fold the orange cream and flour alternately into the butter and egg mixture, about one-third of each at a time.

4 Tip the mixture into the prepared loaf tin and bake in the preheated oven for 45–55 minutes until well risen and a skewer inserted in the centre comes out clean.

5 Cool on a rack for 20 minutes before removing from the tin. Leave until cold, then store in an airtight tin.

Possibly the biscuit I make more than any other, these old-fashioned biscuits can be made by even the youngest child, and when cooking fill the house with that most luscious of scents, butter and vanilla baking. Don't be tempted to squeeze them all on to one tray or baking sheet; they do spread alarmingly.

melting moments

140g butter, softened | 110g caster sugar | 1 teaspoon vanilla extract | 200g self-raising flour | 55g cornflakes, crushed

makes about 20 biscuits

1 Preheat the oven to 200°C/400°F/Gas mark 6.

2 Cream the butter with the sugar. Add the vanilla, then mix in the flour.

3 Spread the cornflakes on to a tray. Take small balls of dough and press them lightly into the cornflakes, making sure both sides are covered.

4 Place these on another baking tray or sheet, well spaced, and cook in the preheated oven for 15–20 minutes. Remove from the oven, and allow the biscuits to cool for 5 minutes before removing from the tray. Leave on a rack until cold, then store in an airtight tin.

Known as 'fairy cakes' when I was a child, the trendy name for these iced delights is now 'cupcakes'. This is definitely an Americanism, where cupcakes have a long and illustrious history. The difference could be in the final icing. Scoop out a circle of cake to make wings, or just load the coloured butter cream on top – the choice, as with the name, is yours.

simply gorgeous fairy cakes

70g butter, softened | **170g caster sugar** | **2 medium eggs, beaten** | **1 teaspoon vanilla extract** | **225g plain flour** | **2 teaspoons baking powder** | **2–4 tablespoons milk**

Extra flavourings (optional) **2 tablespoons hundreds and thousands** | **2 heaped tablespoons chopped glacé cherries** | **2 tablespoons cocoa powder** | **2 tablespoons finely chopped walnuts**

For the butter cream icing **75g butter, softened** | **400g icing sugar, sifted** | **1–2 tablespoons milk** | **several food colourings**

Toppings **cherries, sprinkles, silver balls, nuts etc.**

makes 12–18

1 Preheat the oven to 200°C/400°F/Gas mark 6. Line deep muffin tins with 24 paper cases.

2 Beat the butter and sugar together until light and fluffy. Add the egg and vanilla, and beat well. Sift the flour with the baking powder, then mix this into the mixture in three batches, adding a tablespoon of milk between the batches. Beat for about 30 seconds. The mixture should drop easily from a spoon; if not, add a tablespoon or two more milk. If you want to flavour the cakes, mix in your hundreds and thousands, cherries, cocoa or walnuts.

3 Divide the mixture between the paper cases, filling them about half full. Bake in the oven until cooked through, about 10–15 minutes. Remove from the oven and allow to cool.

4 Make the icing by beating together the butter, icing sugar and milk. Whisk for about 8–10 minutes. Divide between smaller bowls and colour each to your choice.

5 Pile the icing on to the cakes. To make wings, cut a circle from the top of some of the cakes. Fill the hole you've created with a good spoonful of icing. Now cut the reserved circle of cake into two semicircles, and stick these into the icing to form fairy's wings.

A rather different carrot cake this, with tart lemon icing. You can make little marzipan carrots to decorate it if you will.

coconut and carrot loaf cake

200ml sunflower oil, plus extra for greasing | **285g plain flour** | **2 teaspoons baking powder** |
½ teaspoon salt | **225g caster sugar** | **4 large eggs, beaten** | **finely grated zest and juice of 1 large lemon** |
1 teaspoon vanilla extract | **285g finely grated carrot** | **110g desiccated coconut**
For the icing **finely grated zest and juice of 1 large lemon** | **170g caster sugar**

makes 1 loaf

1 Line a 1kg loaf tin with a strip of greaseproof paper, and grease this. Preheat the oven to 180°C/350°F/Gas mark 4.

2 Sift the flour, baking powder and salt together, then add the sugar. In a large bowl beat the eggs, lemon zest and juice, oil and vanilla. Fold in the flour mixture, carrot and coconut.

3 Pour the mixture into the prepared loaf tin, and bake in the preheated oven for 45–55 minutes. The cake is cooked when a skewer inserted in the centre comes out clean.

4 While the cake is cooking, mix the lemon zest and juice into the caster sugar to make the icing.

5 Remove the cake from the oven, prick the top with a skewer or tooth-pick and pour over the icing. When the cake has cooled, remove from the tin and store in an airtight container.

This recipe is infinitely variable, and you can adapt it to use any number of other flavourings: sun-dried tomatoes and grated cheese would be delicious. Yoghurt adds an acidic note that encourages the baking powder to rise even higher; buttermilk has the same effect. Scones are ridiculously easy to make. Once you have made the dough you should get it into the oven as quickly as possible.

red onion and crispy bacon scone ring

110g streaky bacon, cut into small pieces, or lardons | 1 medium red onion, peeled and chopped | 255g plain flour | 2 level teaspoons baking powder | ½ teaspoon celery salt | ¼ teaspoon dry mustard powder | 150g natural yoghurt or 150ml buttermilk | 5 tablespoons sunflower oil | 1 small egg, beaten, to glaze

serves 8

1 Preheat the oven to 220°C/425°F/Gas mark 7.

2 Cook the bacon in a heavy frying pan until the fat runs. Add the onion and cook until both are well coloured. Drain off any excess grease and allow to cool.

3 Sift the flour, baking powder, celery salt and mustard into a bowl, and make a well in the centre. Add the yoghurt or milk and oil, plus the bacon and onion mixture. Mix until the dough is well combined, then turn on to a floured board and knead briefly.

4 Shape into a circle about 18cm across, and place on a baking sheet. Using a blunt knife, mark the dough across the centre to give six portions. Brush with beaten egg to glaze, and bake in the preheated oven for 15–20 minutes, or until well risen and golden brown. The scone should sound hollow if the base is tapped.

5 Allow to cool before storing in an airtight tin. (It freezes well.) Serve split and buttered, stuffed with lettuce and tomatoes or watercress.

beach picnic

A picnic on the beach is surely the best of summer treats: golden sands, sandwiches, flasks of tea and glorious childhood memories. I love to picnic and do so at every opportunity, often taking tea and cake to eat following an after-work swim. We English adore picnics, and at the drop of a hat we grab a basket and Thermos and head for the great outdoors. We don't even really need sunshine. The promise that we can gather together the contents of the refrigerator and take them outside, albeit under an umbrella, is all that is needed to transform a meal into both a feast and an adventure. Will you find the ideal spot? Will you remember the wet wipes, the umbrella, the wine, the corkscrew? All these anxieties are sharpened by glorious anticipation and the unreliability of the English weather. Good picnics, where the sun shines, the water's warm and the day is quarrel-free, are golden moments set in time.

beach picnic

I am a profoundly committed carnivore, but that doesn't mean I don't like non-meat dishes. These cheesy sausages are a great favourite, and they can be made with any tasty, slightly crumbly cheese. The idea is that cheeses that melt well such as Gouda probably won't work, but those that are tricky to cut will. The 'Glamorgan' comes from the fact that traditionally these sausages are made using Welsh cheese. Chopped red chilli adds a certain something, but as this is a family picnic I've left it out.

glamorgan sausages

225g Caerphilly cheese | **170g day-old white breadcrumbs** | **3 tablespoons finely sliced spring onions** | **2 tablespoons chopped parsley** | **3 large eggs** | **sea salt and black pepper** | **flour, for dusting**

To cook **vegetable oil, for deep-frying** | **1 large egg, beaten** | **about 170g plain flour or breadcrumbs**

serves 8

1 Put all the ingredients for the sausages in the bowl of a food processor and season well. Process until the mixture is finely chopped and begins to form a ball. Tip on to a lightly floured board and divide the mixture into eight to ten pieces. Shape these into sausages, lay on baking parchment, cover, then chill for at least 30 minutes.

2 Heat the oil for deep-frying until hot. Dip the sausages in the beaten egg, then roll in flour or breadcrumbs and deep-fry until golden brown on all sides and cooked through. When cooked, drain on absorbent paper, then cool and chill.

Whilst it would be wonderful to be sure that a day on the beach would bring hot sunny weather, with only a necessary hint of breeze to cool the worst excesses of a relentless sun, experience tells me that a Thermos of hot soup is a handy stand-by for thawing out those brave folk who swim in the North Sea.

Heinz tomato soup is a classic, but home-made transcends even Heinz: rich, fresh and without that cloying texture. Light chicken stock can be used to dilute the soup, but I favour water for a picnic: this lets the clear flavours shine and makes the soup more refreshing.

tomato soup

3–4 tablespoons olive oil | 4 medium shallots, peeled and chopped | 2 plump garlic cloves, peeled and crushed | 2kg ripe tomatoes on the vine, roughly chopped (reserve some of the calyxes) | few sprigs of basil or tarragon | caster sugar | sea salt and black pepper | water or stock

serves 8

1 In a large pot, heat the oil, then add the shallot and garlic. Gently stew over a moderate heat until they have softened – they don't need to brown. Add the tomatoes plus the reserved calyxes. Pull the leaves from the herb stems and add the stems to the pot. Reserve the leaves. Season the tomato mixture with about a teaspoon of sugar and about ½ teaspoon salt, plus a grind of pepper. Cover the pan with a lid, and cook the mixture over a very gentle heat until soft and very thick, about 10 minutes.

2 Now comes the boring part. Whizz the mixture, in batches, in a food processor or blender, then rub this purée through a sieve. This removes all the pips, skin and stems, and makes the soup palatable to even the youngest child.

3 In a clean pan, reheat the purée, diluting it to taste with water or stock. Correct the seasoning. When hot, chop the reserved herb leaves, add to the soup and pour into a heated Thermos.

I've developed quite a passion for these chops. I think the real Reform Club cutlets were a little more fancy, with ham chopped into the crumb coating, but I see no need to slavishly copy. You need to trim all the fat from the cutlets; they will be coated and fried and any fat not trimmed will be deeply unappetising. Whenever you coat any food for deep-frying you must season the flour well.

lamb cutlets 'reform' with minted yoghurt sauce

plain flour | **sea salt and black pepper** | **2–3 lamb cutlets per person or more, very well trimmed** | **beaten egg** | **fresh breadcrumbs** | **thyme leaves** | **vegetable oil, for shallow-frying**
For the minted yoghurt sauce **300ml full-fat plain yoghurt or, better yet, Greek yoghurt** | **2 tablespoons chopped fresh mint** | **sea salt and black pepper** | **Tabasco sauce** | **a little ground cumin (optional)**

serves 8

I Season the flour well with salt and pepper. Dip the chops first in this, then in the beaten egg. Mix the breadcrumbs with the thyme leaves, and coat the cutlets with the mixture, pressing on well. Cover and allow the chops to chill for 30 minutes.

2 Shallow-fry the cutlets in hot oil until golden brown on both sides and cooked through. Serve at room temperature with the minted yoghurt sauce. For this, simply mix the yoghurt with the mint, adding salt, pepper, Tabasco and cumin (if using) to taste. (In the absence of fresh mint, a little ready-made mint sauce concentrate works well.)

Bread is easy to make – you must believe me! Home-made bread has an incomparable taste and texture, and can be personalised to suit family idiosyncrasies. Bread rolls are easy to eat on the beach, filling you up and allowing you to run and splash in the sea while you snack. The baked-in filling in these rolls means that each one is ready to be pulled from the ring as needed.

stuffed picnic rolls

I quantity basic bread dough (see page 158)

Filling and topping ingredients **many and various (see below)** | **olive oil** | **coarse salt** | **few sprigs of rosemary**

serves 8

I Mix and knead the dough as described on page 158. Once the dough has doubled in size after its first rising, which takes about I hour, knock it back and knead lightly.

2 Roll out the dough to give a thickness of about Icm.

3 Raid the refrigerator or store cupboard for fillings. You can spread the dough with pesto, sun-dried tomato paste, tapenade, herb-flavoured soft cheese or even butter and Marmite. Scatter on one or two of the following: drained tins of tuna or anchovies, flaked or chopped; grated hard cheese; diced ham; fresh chopped herbs; chopped sun-dried tomatoes; fried sliced or chopped onions; pitted olives; chopped walnuts; or dried fruit.

4 Roll up as for a Swiss roll, then cut into 4cm slices. Place cut-end up in a 20cm springform tin, squeezing all the rolls in. Allow to double in size, covered, for another 40 minutes or so. Meanwhile, preheat the oven to 200°C/400°F/Gas mark 6.

5 Bake for 30–40 minutes. Cool in the tin for 30 minutes, then remove and allow to cool completely before wrapping.

Simple and tasty, all you need from a recipe, the spicy flavours really hold up for outdoor eating. Eat slices in your fingers or, as they do in Spain, stuffed into fresh, crusty bread rolls.

spiced vegetable omelette

6 large eggs | 4 tablespoons chopped parsley or coriander | sea salt and black pepper | 2 tablespoons vegetable oil

For the curry **4 tablespoons vegetable oil | 450g maincrop potatoes, peeled and cut into 2cm dice | 1 medium onion, peeled and finely chopped | 2 garlic cloves, peeled and finely chopped | 1 teaspoon black mustard seeds | ½ teaspoon cumin seeds | ½ teaspoon coriander seeds | 2–3 dried red chillies | sea salt | 200g tinned chopped tomatoes in juice | good handful of baby spinach or chard leaves**

serves 8

1 Make the curry first. Heat the oil in a frying pan and fry the potato, shaking the pan often, until it begins to colour. Add the onion and fry until this, too, takes on some colour. Drain off any excess oil and add the garlic. Using a pestle and mortar, roughly crush the seeds and dried chilli. Add to the pan and stir as the seeds begin to sizzle and pop. Now put in some salt, the tomato and about 150ml water. Bring to the boil. Simmer the mixture for 10 minutes, or until the potato is cooked through and the sauce thick. Now add the spinach and cook until wilted. Let this mixture cool for about 5 minutes.

2 For the omelette, beat the eggs with the parsley or coriander and plenty of salt and pepper. Gently mix in the potato curry.

3 Heat the oil in a frying pan, ideally about 23cm across. Pour in the omelette mix and cook over a moderate heat until the egg sets. Either invert on to a plate and return to the pan to cook the other side or place the frying pan under a hot grill for 3–4 minutes until the top of the omelette is golden. Serve cut into thick slices.

These can be served with the same yoghurt dip/sauce that goes with the lamb (see page 38). Or stir a spoonful of chutney and half a spoonful of curry paste into some Greek yoghurt – sounds odd, but works a treat.

raw vegetable dippers

2 medium carrots, peeled | 10cm piece of cucumber | 1 red pepper, deseeded | 1 yellow pepper, deseeded | 1 medium courgette, trimmed

serves 8

1   Cut the vegetables into 1cm sticks and put into a bowl filled with iced water.

2   Mix the dip ingredients together (see introduction), and spoon into a plastic bowl with a sealed lid. Chill.

3   Just before leaving the house, drain the vegetables, wrap in paper towels, and put into a plastic bag, sealing well. The damp paper keeps the vegetables fresh and can be used as wipes at the picnic. (Slices of melon, seeded and peeled, can be carried in the same way.)

You must have cake on a picnic. This one works well because the brown sugar and coconut release energy more slowly than a refined sugar cake, keeping everyone alert for that last game of beach football.

date and coconut bars

225g butter, plus extra for greasing | **2 large tablespoons golden syrup** | **2 large eggs** | **280g chopped dates** | **280g demerara sugar** | **170g desiccated coconut** | **225g self-raising flour**

serves 8

1 Grease a 30 × 18cm roasting tin, and preheat the oven to 160°C/325°F/Gas mark 3.

2 Melt the butter and syrup together. Allow to cool for 5 minutes, then beat in the eggs. Mix all the dry ingredients in a bowl, then add the egg mixture and stir well. Tip the mixture into the greased roasting tin and press it down evenly.

3 Bake in the preheated oven for 40–45 minutes until risen and golden brown. Allow to cool before slicing into bars.

4 Wrap in a double layer of foil or greaseproof paper for travelling.

fruit
pickers'
high tea

The concept of pick-your-own has had a dramatic impact on the availability of our native and highly perishable summer fruits. The problem is that I am so enthused by the sheer volume of fruit available that I forget the size of both my family and my refrigerator, and end up not just picking 'my own' but also enough to feed a small country town. There is something wonderful about walking into a strawberry field: the scent of berries, the hum of the bees, the joy when a hitherto undiscovered patch of beauties is found .... No wonder then that you just have to keep on picking. To fortify the pickers on their triumphant return, I'm suggesting reviving another lost tradition, that of high tea, a splendid occasion when tables were piled with all manner of dishes, washed down with large cups of tea. A far cry from wafer-thin cucumber sandwiches, the food at a high tea should be robust and easy to eat, but without any hint of blandness.

fruit pickers' high tea

I love corned beef, but know that there are some folk who really can't abide it, so for those friends I make these cakes with hot-smoked salmon. We have two smoke-houses within easy reach of Aldeburgh, but mail order is a fine way to get slightly different ingredients delivered to your home. Oh, the joys of Internet shopping!

corned beef or salmon hash cakes

olive oil or dripping | 1 large onion, peeled and finely chopped | 2 ribs celery, finely chopped |
1 plump garlic clove, peeled and crushed | 1 x 340g tin corned beef or 340g hot-smoked salmon |
450g cold mashed potato | 1 large egg, beaten | 1–2 tablespoons Worcestershire sauce | a few drops of Tabasco
sauce | grated zest of 1 lemon (if using salmon) | 1 fresh red chilli, seeded and chopped (optional) | sea salt and
black pepper | plain flour, for coating

serves 4–6

1 Heat about 3 tablespoons of the oil in a heavy-bottomed frying pan and, when hot, fry the onion, celery and garlic until soft.

2 Meanwhile, if using, chop the corned beef into small pieces. Add the beef to the pan and stir well, breaking the meat down a little with a spatula. If using salmon instead, flake the fish, removing any bones or skin, then add it to the onion mixture when cool.

3 Tip the beef or salmon mixture into a bowl with the mashed potato. Add the egg, and season well with the Worcestershire sauce, Tabasco, lemon zest and chilli (if using), and some salt and pepper, and mix everything together.

4 Shape the mixture into cakes about 7.5cm across and dip into seasoned flour to coat lightly.

5 Fry the hash cakes in a clean pan in 2–3 more tablespoons of oil, turning once or twice, until both sides are well coloured and the cakes are cooked through. Serve the hash cakes with salsa or topped with a fried egg.

Quick to make, these cheesy toasts can be done well in advance of the meal, and they could persuade even the pickiest child to love fish.

smoked haddock toasties

450g smoked haddock | 600ml milk | I bay leaf | 30g butter | 30g plain flour | 110g Cheddar, freshly grated |
sea salt and black pepper | Tabasco sauce | bunch spring onions, finely sliced | 8 slices hot buttered toast

serves 4–6

I Place the haddock, milk and bay leaf in a shallow pan, and bring to the boil. Cover and simmer for 2–3 minutes, then remove the pan from the heat and leave for 5 minutes. Lift the fish out of the milk, reserving the liquid, and allow to cool for 5 minutes. Flake the flesh, discarding all skin and bone. Strain the milk.

2 Make a roux by cooking the butter and flour together until bubbling. Add 300ml of the reserved milk and simmer, whisking, until you have a smooth and thick white sauce, about 2–3 minutes. Add half the cheese and season to taste with pepper and, if needed, a little salt. Add Tabasco to taste. Fold in the fish and the spring onion. This can be done ahead.

3 Just before serving, heat the grill. Spoon some of the haddock mixture on to each slice of toast, then scatter over the remaining cheese. Grill until golden and bubbling. Halve the toast and serve at once.

Salsas can be made with any ripe fruit, including tomatoes, whilst here of course I've used strawberries. This is good with the hash cakes.

strawberry salsa

300g firm, slightly under-ripe strawberries | ½ red onion, peeled and finely chopped | I fresh red chilli, seeded and finely chopped | ½ teaspoon caster sugar | I tablespoon wine vinegar | juice and finely grated zest of I lime | sea salt and black pepper | good handful of coriander leaves or mint, chopped

serves 4–6

I   Dice the strawberries and mix with the red onion, chilli, sugar, vinegar and lime juice and zest. Season with salt and pepper, then taste and add extra seasoning or sugar if needed. Mix in your chosen herb.

2   This salsa can be made up to 6 hours ahead.

This recipe is perfect for any berries that have been squashed. The best tip I can give when it comes to making mousses or cold soufflés is that mixtures to be folded together must have the same consistency. So don't over-whip the cream or egg white, and do let the gelatine mixture set until floppy.

strawberry mousse

900g fresh strawberries | juice of 2 large lemons | 225g caster sugar | I sachet powdered gelatine | 3 large egg whites | 300ml whipping cream | 2 tablespoons rosewater (optional) | rose petals, for decoration

serves 4–6

I   Purée the strawberries, rubbing the mixture through a sieve if you want to remove the seeds.

2   Mix the lemon juice, half the sugar and 4 tablespoons water in a small saucepan, and sprinkle on the gelatine. Allow this to soak for about 10 minutes, then warm the mixture until the sugar and gelatine have dissolved fully. Stir this into the strawberry purée, mixing well. Allow this to cool and begin to thicken and set.

3   Now whisk the egg whites until they hold soft peaks, then whisk in the remaining sugar and beat until you have a stiffish meringue. Whisk the cream and rosewater (if using) together until floppy.

4   Fold the cream into the strawberry purée, then fold this mixture into the meringue. Pour into a large glass bowl and leave to set. Decorate with rose petals.

These light shortcakes are much like traditional scones, but slightly sweeter and so quick to make. Cream replaces the butter, so there's no rubbing in. I like to add some finely chopped thyme or rosemary, or even lavender flowers to the mix. As with all baking-powder breads, the oven must be hot before you start to mix.

crisp raspberry shortcakes

300g plain flour | **2 teaspoons baking powder** | **½ teaspoon salt** | **45g caster sugar, plus extra for dredging** | **1 teaspoon finely chopped rosemary or thyme leaves, or 1 teaspoon whole lavender flowers** | **300ml double cream** | **2–4 tablespoons milk, plus a little extra for brushing** | **flour, for dusting**
To serve **whipped cream** | **raspberries**

serves 4–6

1 Preheat the oven to 200°C/400°F/Gas mark 6.

2 Mix the dry ingredients and the herbs together in a bowl. Add the cream and enough milk to form a stiff dough.

3 Tip on to a lightly floured board and pat or roll to a thickness of about 2.5cm. Cut into 8cm circles and place on a floured baking sheet. Brush the tops with a little extra milk, and dust liberally with sugar.

4 Bake in the preheated oven for 10–12 minutes until well risen and light brown. Allow to cool on a rack.

5 Split open the shortcakes and fill with whipped cream and raspberries.

Delicious warm, it tastes just as good at room temperature, but as with most summer fruit chilling dulls and deadens the flavour. Use good wine for this dessert 'soup'.

red fruit soup

400ml fruity red wine such as Cabernet Sauvignon or Shiraz | 1.5kg assorted red fruit (cherries, raspberries, blackcurrants, redcurrants, strawberries, blueberries) | 170g caster sugar, or to taste

serves 4–6

1 Put the wine into a large saucepan and add the 'tougher' fruit (cherries, currants, blueberries). Turn up the heat, stir in the sugar and cook for 4–5 minutes. The mixture should barely simmer.

2 Remove from the heat and spoon into a glass serving dish. Add the remaining berries – the strawberries cut to size – and allow to cool.

Possibly the simplest strawberry dessert of all.

berries in champagne

ripe strawberries | cassis | champagne

1 Cut very ripe, scented berries in half and divide between deep wine goblets. Add a measure of cassis and top up with champagne! The cassis can be home-made and the sparkling wine English. I love Moonshine from the Leaping Hare vineyard in Suffolk.

Choose ripe, even slightly crushed, berries here. This really should be used within a few hours of making, as the juice will begin to ferment in warm weather.

strawberry crush

450g strawberries | caster sugar | fizzy mineral water | ice cubes

serves 6

1 Crush the berries, either with a fork or in a food processor, adding sugar to taste.

2 Place about 2 tablespoons of the purée into a deep glass and add mineral water and ice. The mixture will froth, so top up with water after a few moments.

Blackcurrants are said to cool the blood and relieve joint pain, so this tea might be just the thing after a sun-drenched day in the strawberry fields!

blackcurrant tea

serves 4–6   **110g blackcurrants | 30g caster sugar, plus extra to taste | small handful young blackcurrant leaves**

1 Mash the currants with the sugar, add the leaves, and pour over 1.2 litres boiling water. Allow to infuse for 5 minutes, then serve, straining the tea through a fine sieve. Add extra sugar to taste.

midsummer barbecue

Think twice before trusting even those you love with the
barbecue tongs. A personality change comes over folk when
they hold them. Grilling food is an art: the heat must be high
and the cook attentive, but you must leave the food to cook.
Light the fire at least 30 minutes before you need it, and have
plenty of coals to top up the barbecue if you intend to cook for
a crowd. Many types of fish cook well on a barbecue. Robust
fish such as tuna or swordfish steaks are excellent if they are
marinated first. Salmon steaks just need seasoning, trout can
be stuffed with fresh herbs, and mackerel are transformed by
cooking over coals. Whole fillets of beef or boned legs of lamb
take about 40 minutes over moderate coals. The good news
about cooking such joints is they permit more room for error,
allowing a better ratio of meat to char if concentration slips
and the cooking goes a little awry.

midsummer barbecue

Home-made burgers are delicious, and you know exactly what has gone into them! Use fairly lean minced beef or try minced lamb seasoned with finely chopped rosemary and mint.

really great hamburgers

450g lean minced beef | **½ large onion, peeled and finely chopped** | **2 tablespoons double cream or thick yoghurt** | **1 tablespoon chopped chives** | **1 tablespoon chopped parsley** | **1 small garlic clove, crushed** | **sea salt and black pepper**

To serve **buns or pitta** | **sliced onion and relish**

serves 6

1 Mix all the ingredients together well, kneading the mixture with your hands. Burgers need lots of seasoning, so add about ½ teaspoon salt, plus a few grinds of pepper.

2 Shape the meat into patties about 7–10cm in diameter and about 2.5cm thick. Cook on a barbecue grill for about 3–5 minutes each side, until cooked through. (The burgers can be basted with a barbecue sauce towards the end of cooking.)

3 Serve in buns or pitta or home-made bread pockets with sliced onion and relish.

The good thing about kebabs is that, whilst they do take a little time to prepare, they are simple to cook, serve and eat, all the hard work having been done earlier.

When shopping for meat to be grilled you should choose cuts that are both reasonably tender and that have some integral fat. This will baste the meat from the inside as it cooks and ensure a moist, tender meal. A good example of this is the ubiquitous chicken breast which, whilst tender, is too dry to grill successfully on a barbecue. Chicken thigh meat on the other hand grills well, with a delicious melting texture and lots of flavour. A note here: please do buy free-range chicken; the horrors done in the name of cheap food are especially dire when it comes to chicken production.

Allow about 140g meat per person; 185g for those with large appetites.

marinated mixed meat kebabs

800g (trimmed weight) steak, pork fillet, lamb or skinned chicken thigh meat

For the marinade **1 shallot, peeled and finely chopped** | **2–3 tablespoons olive oil** | **finely grated zest of 1 orange** | **1 garlic clove, peeled and crushed** | **2 tablespoons finely chopped thyme, rosemary, sage or other herb** | **freshly ground black pepper** | **dash of Tabasco sauce**

To finish **2 red peppers** | **2–3 medium courgettes** | **4 red onions** | **12 button mushrooms** | **2 medium aubergines** | **sea salt** | **lemon and orange quarters**

serves 6

1 Cut the meat to give largish chunks, about 3cm is ideal. Mix the marinade ingredients together and let the meat sit in this, covered, in the refrigerator for anything from an hour to a day.

2 Cut the vegetables into cubes of a similar size to the meat.

3 Thread the cubes, alternating meat and vegetables, on to wooden or metal skewers, but make sure the wooden skewers have been soaking in water for at least half an hour to avoid burning. Brush with the excess marinade and sprinkle generously with salt.

4 Cook on a well-heated barbecue, turning as needed, until the meat is cooked to your liking. Do remember that chicken and pork must be cooked through. Squeeze lemon and orange juice over the cooked kebabs and serve.

This butter is wonderfully versatile. Spread it on bread, let it melt over grilled meat and fish, or toss it into new potatoes or lightly cooked summer vegetables. It can be rolled in clingfilm and keeps well if frozen.

chilli and herb spiked garlic butter

1 fresh red chilli | **225g lightly salted butter** | **handful of coriander, chervil, tarragon or parsley leaves** | **freshly ground black pepper** | **finely grated zest of 1 lime** | **2 plump garlic cloves, peeled**

serves 6

1   If you wish, remove the pith and seeds from the chilli to lessen the heat.

2   Place all the ingredients in a food processor, and whizz until everything is finely chopped and well blended. The butter can be served as is in a dish, or prepared as below.

3   Prepare a double layer of clingfilm about 30cm square. Scrape the butter on to the clingfilm, then roll up to form a sausage. Tie off one end, then squeeze the butter up to give a roll about 15cm long. Chill before cutting into slices.

a note about barbecuing chicken

No matter that there are wonderful alternatives, for many a charred chicken drumstick is the epitome of a summer barbecue.

Coated in sticky tomato-and-sugar-rich barbecue sauce, children love them, goes the popular myth, but they really are about the most difficult thing to cook properly on a heat source as temperamental as a barbecue grill. Chicken must be cooked through and my experience is that children hate anything dry or burnt, so how does one ensure succulence and safety? My answer to this dilemma is to par-boil the chicken for about 15 minutes, about an hour before you grill it.

This pre-cooking, simmering in water with seasoning vegetables, ensures the meat is cooked through and moist. Drain well, then brush with barbecue sauce before finishing on the grill. (The cooking water will give you a light stock, so don't discard it.)

Why relish and not salsa? Well, this side dish is lightly cooked to thicken it, but not cooked long enough to preserve it.

fresh herb and tomato relish

2 tablespoons olive oil | I large red onion, peeled and chopped | 2 garlic cloves, peeled and crushed | 500g ripe tomatoes | 3 tablespoons light muscovado sugar | 3 tablespoons wine vinegar | I teaspoon fennel seeds, crushed | I teaspoon salt and a good quantity of ground black pepper | 2–3 tablespoons chopped coriander, tarragon or basil

serves 6

I   Heat the oil in a saucepan, and cook the onion and garlic over a low heat until softened.

2   Meanwhile, prepare the tomatoes. I leave the skins on for a chunky relish, but if you have a real aversion to tomato skin, do peel them. Cut the flesh into I cm cubes, removing any stringy core.

3   Add the tomato to the onion and garlic, along with the sugar, vinegar, fennel and salt and pepper. Cook over a moderate heat for about 5–7 minutes, until the mixture is thickish – it will thicken more as it cools.

4   Allow to cool, then stir in the fresh chopped herbs. Serve with hamburgers and sausages.

Hot bread eaten from the grill is one of life's pleasures. This recipe is a variation on my basic bread recipe, and, unlike the other breads, it doesn't need a second rising. I add all sorts of stuff to flavour it: crushed chillies, dried herbs, crushed whole spices such as coriander or cumin, finely sliced spring onion and chopped fresh herbs. Children can be co-opted to do the kneading and rolling, but the cooking should be well supervised.

barbecue flat breads

1 recipe basic bread dough (see page 158) | **flavouring to taste (as above)**

serves 6

I Make the dough as described on page 158, but adding only about 2 tablespoons of the olive oil at first. Knead the dough for about 5 minutes. Put the ball of dough back into the bowl, smear the remaining oil over the surface and leave until doubled in size. On a hot summer's day this will take about 45 minutes.

2 Prepare the flavourings to taste: I use about a teaspoon of each of two spices, ½ teaspoon chilli flakes and a tablespoon chopped herb.

3 Knock back the dough, kneading the flavourings in well. Divide the dough into rounds about the size of a golf ball, then roll them as thinly as possible. The thinner the better, as this bread is being cooked on the grill.

4 Place the flat bread on the barbecue, then leave it alone until large bubbles appear. Now turn over and cook the other side. Ideally there should be small slightly charred areas. Not burnt – charred! If the bread seems doughy inside, split open and cook doughy side down for a few moments. Eat at once, split and buttered, or torn into pieces with a dip.

I have a terracotta wood oven next to my barbecue, and should you have the space and inclination I do urge you to get one. You light the fire in the oven and leave it for about 30 minutes before you cook – much the same idea as preheating a normal oven. The similarities end there, as the heat in a wood oven is both dry and intense. I find fish is quite wonderful cooked in this way.

cod roasted in the wood oven

750g centre cut of cod or salmon | **sea salt and black pepper** | **olive oil** | **fennel sticks or rosemary stems** | **I red onion, peeled and finely sliced** | **couple of whole garlic heads**

serves 6

I Have the fishmonger scale the fish, then wash it well. Pat it dry, then season inside and out.

2 Pour about 2–3 tablespoons oil into a terracotta dish that fits into the oven (that's important!). Place some of the fennel sticks or rosemary over the base of the dish, then put the fish on top. Tuck more herbs into the fish and some of the onion slices. Slice the garlic heads in half through the 'equator', and place these cut-side down in some oil on the base of the dish. Drizzle more oil over the fish, scatter on more salt and pepper, and the remaining onion and herbs.

3 Cook in the hot oven for 15–20 minutes. (For a conventional oven, cook for about 25–30 minutes at 200°C/400°F/Gas mark 6.) Allow to rest for 5 minutes before serving. (You can use the remaining heat in the oven to cook the fruit crisp on page 68.)

For a salad to be dressed with the following raspberry vinaigrette, any fresh leaves picked from the garden work well. For city dwellers I suggest either a farmers' market or a couple of packets of mixed salad from the supermarket!

raspberry vinaigrette

raspberry vinegar (see page 136) | olive oil or groundnut oil | sea salt and black pepper

I   The usual proportions for a vinaigrette are 6 tablespoons oil to 3–4 of vinegar. Season as always with salt and pepper, but to keep the flavour of this vinaigrette clean I would omit the oft-included ingredients of garlic and mustard.

On the heathland just outside Aldeburgh is a blueberry farm. This is one of those glorious bits of serendipity that make life delightful, for when living in the United States I learned to love blueberries. Whilst I will eat imported fruit, I do prefer to support British producers, so think how thrilled I am to be able to support genuinely local growers whilst still indulging my greed for these delicious berries. Aldeburgh blueberries are enormous, about the size of 20p pieces, and are wonderful eaten fresh. My love for pies, fruit crisps and pancakes means that I often cook them. A 'crisp' is similar to a crumble, but with a lighter touch and often, as here, with the addition of nuts. This is my favourite summer recipe, buttery and rich.

blueberry and nectarine crisp

6 ripe nectarines | 450g blueberries | juice of I lemon | I tablespoon brandy | I tablespoon plain flour | 2 tablespoons caster sugar
For the topping **110g blanched almonds | 170g plain flour | 85g caster sugar | I teaspoon ground cinnamon | 170g butter, softened, plus extra for greasing**

serves 6

I Preheat the oven to 190°C/375°F/Gas mark 5.

2 Cut the nectarines into quarters, removing the stones, then cut these quarters into eighths. Place these and the blueberries in a greased ovenproof dish. Mix the lemon juice with the brandy, and pour over the fruit. Now sift together the flour and sugar, and sprinkle this over the fruit. Toss everything lightly together.

3 To make the topping, put the almonds into a food processor and whizz until finely chopped. Add the remaining topping ingredients and whizz until the mixture resemble breadcrumbs.

4 Spoon the topping evenly over the fruit and bake in the preheated oven for 45 minutes, or until the top is lightly browned and the fruit soft.

5 Serve warm with cream, crème fraîche or crème fraîche ice-cream (see page 157).

raspberry pimms

170g raspberries | fresh mint leaves | 150ml Pimm's | 100ml elderflower cordial (see page 17) | lemonade

serves 6

1 Half fill a large jug with ice. Add the raspberries and some mint leaves. Stir well. Now add the Pimm's and, if you have it, elderflower cordial.

2 Top up with cold lemonade and stir once more. Serve in tall glasses, diluting with extra lemonade according to taste.

shellfish supper

I love shellfish. Some of my earliest memories are of shrimping and crabbing with my father along the beaches of Old Hunstanton. These days I'm more of a consumer than a hunter-gatherer, but I still eat almost all types of shellfish. I do draw the line at whelks (too chewy) and cockles (too sandy), but for the rest – let the feasting begin! I am not suggesting here that you serve all these dishes for your shellfish supper; such a meal would be dreadfully rich and a little ill balanced. Choose two or three, and remember that shellfish works better with wine than mixed drinks, so this is not the meal to serve with cocktails.

All shellfish should be cooked while still alive, so it is very important to know your source. When cooking mussels or opening oysters you must reject any that you think are dead. The ill effects are not worth the economy.

shellfish supper

By midsummer, tomatoes will be ripe and rich in flavour, and their combination here with shellfish and chilli evokes the Mediterranean. Mussels grow all round our coast, and are available for most of the year, and this is my favourite way of cooking them. Spaghetti is not perhaps a traditional English dish, but we do have the largest dried pasta factory in the United Kingdom quite close by in Norfolk.

spaghetti with mussels and chilli

1.5kg clean mussels, beards removed | 1kg ripe tomatoes | sea salt and black pepper | 340g dried spaghetti | 2 shallots, peeled and chopped | 4 tablespoons good olive oil | 2 plump garlic cloves, peeled and crushed | 1–2 dried chillies, crushed | handful of parsley, chopped | finely grated zest of 1 lemon

serves 4

1 Wash the mussels, discarding any dead ones. Skin the tomatoes by covering with boiling water for 2 minutes, then draining and slipping off the skins. Roughly chop the tomatoes when cool enough to handle.

2 Fill a pan two-thirds full of cold water, bring to the boil, then add a handful of salt and return to the boil. I find a large saucepan or enamelled casserole dish works well. Once the water is boiling for the second time, throw in the pasta, stir well, then cook at a full boil for the time stated on the packet. There is no need to use oil when cooking pasta – simply keep the water boiling and stir from time to time. Test the pasta about 2 minutes before it should be ready by removing a piece and biting into it. You want there to be a slight chalky core. Drain, reserving about 300ml of the cooking water.

3 In a deep frying pan, fry the shallot in the olive oil until soft, then add the garlic, chilli and tomato, cooking for about 3–4 minutes over a moderate heat. Now toss the pasta with this mixture and replace in the cooking pot.

4 Add about half of the reserved water, then place the mussels on top. Return the pan to the heat and cover. Cook over a brisk heat until all the mussels are open, tossing the pasta and shellfish together, using two long spoons, from time to time. If it dries out, add the remaining reserved water. Season the dish with extra salt and pepper, scatter over the parsley and lemon zest, and serve at once.

Serve the potted shellfish with crisp Melba toast (see below)

a trio of potted shellfish

For the shrimps **1.2 litres tiny brown shrimps | 225g butter | finely grated zest of 1 lemon | few drops of lemon juice | Tabasco sauce | sea salt | freshly grated nutmeg**
For the crab **170g butter | 2 dressed crabs | 1 tablespoon chopped tarragon (optional) | finely grated zest of 1 lemon | sea salt and black pepper | Tabasco sauce**
For the lobster **meat from 1 small cooked lobster | 170g butter | sea salt and black pepper | Tabasco sauce | grated zest of 1 lemon | some finely chopped chives or shredded basil leaves**

serves 4

1   Peel the shrimps. (The shells can be saved and used to make a shellfish stock.)

2   Melt the butter, adding the lemon zest and a few drops of juice, a good shake of Tabasco, and some salt and nutmeg. Taste to ensure the butter is well seasoned and the flavours balance. Remember that when cold the flavours will be less pronounced.

3   Now add the shrimps and cook them gently in the butter for 1 minute. Pour the mixture into a small dish and leave to set. Chill before serving with crusty brown bread. Potted shrimps can be topped with clarified butter to give an airtight seal.

crab
Melt the butter and add the dressed brown and white crab meat, breaking it down gently with a fork. Remove from the heat and stir in the seasonings to taste. Pot as above.

lobster
Chop the lobster meat very finely. This is best done on a board with a knife. Now melt the butter, add the lobster meat, and proceed as for crab.

melba toast
I find it best to use a ready-sliced loaf for Melba toast. Try to choose one of the better-quality loaves, ideally cut medium-thick. First toast the bread lightly on both sides. Now cut off the crusts, then slice through the middle of the toast giving two thin slices, both toasted on one side. Lay the slices on a baking sheet and bake in a coolish oven at 150°C/300°F/Gas mark 2 for about 30 minutes, or until crisp and dry.

I've been known, when in Maine, to eat two lobsters at a sitting. North Sea lobsters are denser of flesh and so two would need real commitment. One per person, each weighing 450g, is about right if the budget allows. The meat on these lobsters will be sweeter than on heavyweight monsters of 1 kilo or over, so my top limit for a North Sea lobster is about 750g. I'd serve half a lobster as part of a meal that contained other shellfish.

grilled lobster with chilli herb butter

I   Buy lobsters freshly cooked from your fishmonger. Place the lobster on a board, spreading the tail out. Look for the cross mark on the back of the lobster just behind the head. Starting there, and using a sharp knife, cut the lobster in half through the shell towards the tail. Turn, then finish cutting towards the head. Open the lobster and at the tip of the head you will find a stomach sac (it looks a bit like clingfilm). Remove both halves of this, plus their contents. That's all there is to dressing a lobster – easy, really. Using a hammer, crack the shell of the large legs, but leave them whole. Claws can be cracked at the table using nut crackers or cute lobster-shaped crackers, or you can simply suck the meat out.

2   About 20 minutes before serving, heat a grill or barbecue and, when hot, grill the lobster flesh-side up for about 5 minutes: you don't want to dry the meat; just warm it through and gently char it.

3   Serve immediately with a slice of chilli herb butter (see page 62) melting over the meat, and chips and salad alongside.

I don't make chips often, but when I do they must be perfect. Always use fresh oil. Groundnut oil gives the best results when deep-frying – especially if you wish to avoid the house smelling like a chip shop. Keep the bottle the oil came in, and when cool decant the oil back and throw it away. A pan full of deep fat will encourage you to cook egg and chips with disastrous consequences in the wardrobe department.

perfect chips with garlic mayonnaise

4 large main-crop potatoes (Cara or Desirée are best) | **groundnut oil, for deep-frying** | **sea salt**
For the mayonnaise **150ml olive oil** | **150ml groundnut oil** | **1 teaspoon Dijon mustard** | **1 tablespoon white wine vinegar** | **1 large egg** | **2–3 plump garlic cloves, peeled and mashed to a purée with salt** | **sea salt and black pepper** | **Tabasco sauce to taste**

serves 4

1 Peel the potatoes and cut into even-sized chips. (Fashions change, and thick, straight chips are being served at the moment.) Rinse the chips well in cold water to wash away the loose starch, then dry on kitchen paper. Heat the oil to 160°C/320°F (the easiest way to test this is to check that a cube of white bread will brown in about 1 minute), and fry the chips in small batches for 4–5 minutes, until they soften but are still pale in colour. Remove the chips from the oil, then turn the heat up to 190°C/375°F (when the bread browns in about 20 seconds). Fry the chips again in small batches until they are crisp and golden brown.

2 Drain on kitchen paper, sprinkle with sea salt and serve with the mayonnaise.

garlic mayonnaise

When you make mayonnaise in a food processor or blender, you will need to use the whole egg; if you make it by hand, you just use the yolk. Extra virgin olive oil, the one most of us keep in the kitchen these days, is too strongly flavoured for this mayonnaise, so I've used half olive and half groundnut oil.

Mix the oils. Put the mustard, vinegar, egg, garlic and a little seasoning into the goblet of a food processor, and whizz until smooth. Now, with the motor running, pour in the oil, very slowly at first, then in a thin stream until the mayonnaise starts to thicken. Chill the mayonnaise until needed.

Rather a sophisticated type of fish cake, these crab cakes are wonderfully light and tasty. Handle them with care, as they are a little fragile, and serve with a green salad tossed with a light dressing. The leftover brown meat can be used in the potted crab recipe on page 74. If you're serving mayo with the chips you could serve a salsa with these crab cakes.

crab cakes with tartare sauce

30g butter | **30g plain flour** | **300ml creamy milk** | **I large egg yolk** | **sea salt and black pepper** | **Tabasco sauce** | **225g white crab meat (about the amount of meat you get from I large or 2 medium dressed crabs)** | **a little chopped tarragon** | **I tablespoon chopped parsley** | **2 spring onions, finely sliced** | **1–2 tablespoons lemon juice** | **110g fresh white breadcrumbs** | **plain flour, for dusting** | **vegetable oil, for shallow-frying**
For the tartare sauce **250ml mayonnaise** | **I tablespoon capers, finely chopped** | **2 tablespoons small cornichons (gherkins), finely chopped** | **½ sweet onion or I shallot, peeled and finely chopped** | **sea salt and black pepper** | **Tabasco sauce to taste**

serves 4

I   Start by making a thick white sauce. Melt the butter in a saucepan and stir in the flour. Cook the roux for 2–3 minutes, then add the milk. Whisk well and simmer until you have a very thick smooth sauce. Allow it to cool. Once the sauce is cold, beat in the egg yolk and season well with salt, pepper, and Tabasco to taste. Stir in the crab meat, herbs and spring onion. Add the lemon juice and enough breadcrumbs to give a firmish mixture. If possible, leave in the refrigerator for 30 minutes, covered, to allow the flavours to develop.

2   Take about a heaped tablespoon of the chilled mixture and form into round patties on a well-floured board. Heat a non-stick frying pan, add about 1–2 tablespoons oil and fry the crab cakes until golden brown on both sides, about 5–8 minutes in all. Serve at once.

tartare sauce

This should be a whispering rather than a shouting sauce, i.e. the bits should be close enough to whisper rather than shout across the void, so when mixing start with half the mayo, adding more if needed. Mix everything together, seasoning well with salt, pepper, and Tabasco to taste. Spoon it into a serving bowl.

Rhubarb and strawberries are a match made in heaven. Each fruit, although delicious alone, is enhanced by the marriage. The one drawback to the mix is that both are rather wet, so the pie may ooze juice. Don't panic, most will evaporate in the cooking.

strawberry and rhubarb rough fruit pi

170g butter | 55g lard | 340g plain flour | pinch of salt | 1 large beaten egg, plus extra to glaze | caster sugar, for sprinkling

For the filling **1kg rhubarb | 500g strawberries, hulled | 1 tablespoon plain flour | 55g caster sugar**

serves 6–8

1 Make the pastry about 20 minutes before making the pie, and let it rest in a coolish place. Refrigerating the pastry will make it more likely to crack.

2 I use a food processor to rub the fat into the flour and salt, but it can be done by hand. If using the processor, use short bursts of power, processing until the mixture looks like coarse breadcrumbs. Tip these into a large mixing bowl, then, using a knife, stir in the beaten egg and sufficient cold water to get the crumbs to stick together. Gently knead it into a ball. Wrap in clingfilm and allow to rest for 20 minutes.

3 Preheat the oven to 190°C/375°F/Gas mark 5. To start the filling, cut the rhubarb into 2.5cm pieces and, if necessary, slice the strawberries in half. Mix the flour and sugar together, then toss the fruit in this.

4 Line a baking sheet with baking parchment, then roll the pastry out to give a circle about 40cm across and arrange this on the baking sheet – the edges will flop over the sides of the sheet. Pile the fruit mixture on to the centre of the pastry circle, then bring up the sides. The pastry will wrap round the fruit, leaving a gap in the middle. Brush the pie with beaten egg and sprinkle generously with caster sugar.

5 Bake for about 40 minutes, or until the fruit is soft and the pastry a rich golden brown. Cool for 10 minutes before carefully sliding on to a serving plate. Serve warm with cream.

To offset the richness of all this shellfish, I would suggest a crisply flavoured home-made lemonade. White wine of course is excellent, but lemonade is a road-friendly alternative.

real lemonade

110g caster sugar | finely grated zest and juice of 4 well-scrubbed lemons
To serve mineral water | ice | I lime, finely sliced

makes ½ litre concentrate

I Place the sugar and 300ml water in a saucepan and heat, stirring, until the sugar dissolves. Simmer for 2–3 minutes. Add the lemon zest and juice to the syrup, and store in a stoppered sterilised bottle.

2 To serve, dilute to taste with chilled mineral water, then add ice and lime slices.

VISITORS

BATTING

WKTS

cricket
club tea

Cricket on the village green is one of the outstanding images of an English summer. The grass is perfect, the whites spotless and the batsmen both fearless and handsome. Well, I can dream, but at least the tea will not disappoint. For whether to nourish tired players or to while away the long hours when rain has stopped play, cricket teas are an all-important part of the game. I'm sure there might even be an element of competition between clubs to provide a tea that impresses the visiting side; the recipes that follow should help.

A cricket tea should offer hearty fare. While finely cut cucumber sandwiches might do for the spectators, batsmen and outfielders will need a more substantial meal, so a pie or two, plenty of good tasty sandwiches, some light-as-air scones and a cake should fit the bill nicely.

cricket club tea

This is much easier than you might think, and a home-made pork pie looks magnificent on the table. Don't panic over the pastry: no light touch needed, no rubbing in, just mix in a bowl and leave to cool. If the first time you roll it out it's too fragile to lift, let it cool for a little longer. Should you have a mincer, mince the meat, which gives a slightly better texture to the pie. Serve with home-made piccalilli (see page 139).

raised pork pie

450g plain flour, plus extra for dusting | **1 teaspoon salt** | **120ml each of milk and water** | **170g lard** | **egg wash, to glaze**

For the filling **790g trimmed lean pork** | **110g streaky bacon, rinded** | **4–5 fresh sage leaves, torn** | **good pinch each of ground mace and allspice** | **sea salt and black pepper**

serves 8–10

1 First make the pastry. Sift the flour with the salt into a large bowl, and make a well in the centre. Put the milk, water and lard into a saucepan, and heat until the lard melts. Bring the mixture to the boil, then pour into the well in the flour. Beat the mixture with a wooden spoon until you have a smooth dough. Turn out on to a lightly floured board and, when cool, knead lightly. Return to the bowl and cover with a folded towel to keep warm.

2 Roughly dice the pork and bacon, then place in a food processor with the sage, mace and allspice, and lots of salt and pepper. Whizz the mixture in short bursts until it is roughly chopped and well combined.

3 Break off two-thirds of the dough and roll to give a circle large enough to line a greased and lined 15 x 7.5cm springform tin. Place the pastry in the tin and press in the filling. Roll out the remaining pastry to form a top, and cover the pie, sealing and crimping the edges. Cut a steam vent, decorate with leaves rolled from the trimmings, and brush with egg. Chill for 30 minutes. Meanwhile, preheat the oven to 200°C/400°F/Gas mark 6. Bake for 20 minutes, then turn down the heat to 180°C/350°F/Gas mark 4 and cook the pie for a further 2 hours. Cool completely on a rack before removing from the tin.

5 If you want jelly in your pie, pour a little warm jellied chicken stock (see page 159) in through the steam vent when the pie is cold, and refrigerate until set.

Light-as-air pies will feed the inner man without prejudicing the fielding. Buying pastry is perfectly fine: time is precious, so don't feel guilty. Pasties can be made larger or smaller as the mood takes you.

salmon pasties

I packet ready-made puff or shortcrust pastry, or home-made shortcrust pastry (see page 158) |
beaten egg, to glaze | sesame seeds
For the filling 55g basmati rice | 340g boneless, skinless salmon, finely chopped | I red onion, peeled and finely
chopped | 2 tablespoons roughly chopped tarragon | 2 tablespoons natural yoghurt or crème fraîche | sea salt
and black pepper

makes about 20 I Preheat the oven to 200°C/400°F/Gas mark 6.

2 For the filling, put the rice in a pan with plenty of salted water and boil for 7 minutes. Drain well and allow to cool. Fold the salmon into the cooled rice along with the onion, tarragon, yoghurt and seasoning.

3 Roll out the pastry until about as thick as a 50p piece, then cut out 10cm circles – I made about 20.

4 Pile about a heaped dessertspoon of filling on each circle, then brush the edges with water or beaten egg. Fold the pastry over to give half-moons, pressing the edges well to seal. Brush the tops of the pasties with beaten egg, and scatter on sesame seeds. Chill, covered, for about 10 minutes if you like.

5 Place on a baking sheet and cook in the preheated oven for 12–15 minutes, or until golden brown. Cool on a rack before serving.

The knack of telling how well done a roast is has troubled cooks through the ages. I use a time-honoured method where I take a cold skewer, insert it into the centre of the meat, count to ten, then touch it carefully to my lip. Cold means the meat is uncooked; tepid rare; warm medium; hot cooked through. Always rest meat for 15 minutes before carving. When cooking meat to be served cold, you can err slightly on the side of rare.

roast beef sandwich with fresh horseradish

granary bread | **soft butter** | **rare roast beef, thinly sliced** | **watercress**
For the horseradish cream **grated fresh horseradish** | **100ml double cream, whipped** | **squeeze of lemon juice** |
Tabasco sauce | **sea salt and black pepper**

I   Beat the horseradish into the cream, seasoning well with lemon juice, Tabasco, salt and pepper. Make this as early as possible, as the flavours do develop when left to sit.

2   Butter the bread, lay on a generous helping of beef, top with the horseradish cream, then watercress, and finally another slice of buttered bread.

pesto, avocado and chicken breast
Use the pesto as a spread, filling the sandwich with slices of poached chicken breast and avocado.

grilled vegetables
Fill crusty rolls with griddled slices of aubergine, courgette, onion and red pepper.

herbed egg salad and tomato
Finely chop hard-boiled eggs with a couple of spoonfuls of capers and a big bunch of parsley. Season well and use with finely sliced ripe tomatoes to fill white rolls.

curried cream cheese and alfalfa
Beat some cream or curd cheese with a spoonful of medium curry paste and a larger spoonful of mango chutney. Taste and add seasoning, then spread on granary bread and top with alfalfa or cress sprouts.

Rather different from the usual fruited scones, dried cherries add a tart, chewy element. Serve these scones with clotted cream and cherry preserve. As ever, the trick for light, airy scones is to have the oven heated ready and not to spend too long rolling and cutting – speed is of the essence.

dried cherry scones

225g plain flour, plus extra for dusting | 2 level teaspoons baking powder | ½ teaspoon salt | 55g butter | 55g dried cherries | 150ml milk, plus extra for brushing

makes 8–10

1 Preheat the oven to 220°C/425°F/Gas mark 7.

2 Sift the flour with the baking powder and salt, then rub in the butter. Add the cherries, then the milk, mixing to give a softish dough. Turn this out on to a floured board and roll to about 2.5cm thick. Cut out the scones, re-rolling the trimmings, then place on a baking sheet and brush with a little more milk.

3 Bake in the preheated oven for 10–15 minutes. Cool and serve split with cream and jam.

Classic cakes such as these are a wonderful British tea-time tradition.

orange layer cake

170g butter, plus extra for greasing | **170g caster sugar** | **finely grated zest of a well-scrubbed orange** |
3 large eggs | **juice of ½ orange** | **200g plain flour, plus extra for dusting** | **2 level teaspoons baking powder**
To finish **300ml double cream** | **juice of ½ orange** | **3–4 tablespoons Seville orange marmalade** |
icing sugar, for dusting

makes 1 cake

1 Preheat the oven to 180°C/350°F/Gas mark 4. Line, grease and flour two 18cm sandwich tins.

2 Beat the butter, sugar and orange zest together until light and fluffy. Whisk the eggs together with the juice, and add to the butter and sugar a little at a time, beating constantly. If the mixture splits, add a couple of tablespoons of flour. Sift the flour with the baking powder and fold this in.

3 Divide the mixture between the prepared tins, and bake in the preheated oven for 25–30 minutes, or until the cakes are well risen, golden brown and pulling slightly away from the sides of the tins. Remove and cool for 5 minutes before removing from the tins and cooling on a rack.

4 When the cakes are cold, whip the cream until almost stiff, then mix in the orange juice and the marmalade. Use this mixture to sandwich the layers together. Dust with icing sugar and store in a cool place until needed.

This is a delicious chewy mixture of two favourite flavours.

apricot and oat bars

225g porridge oats | 85g plain flour | 170g soft brown sugar | ½ teaspoon bicarbonate of soda |
170g butter, melted | 350g apricot jam

makes 18–20 bars

1 Preheat the oven to 180°C/350°F/Gas mark 4.

2 Mix the oats, flour, sugar and bicarbonate together, then stir in the melted butter. Press half of this mixture into the base of a 30 × 18 × 2.5cm tin. Spread the apricot jam over this, then carefully scatter the remaining mixture over the top.

3 Bake in the preheated oven for 25–30 minutes, or until golden brown. Allow to cool before slicing into bars.

There are many ways to make iced tea. This is mine.

iced tea

2 teaspoons tea leaves, or more according to taste | **3 tablespoons honey**

To serve **lemon juice** | **ice** | **mint leaves**

makes 1.5 litres

I   Pour 1.7 litres boiling water over the tea leaves and allow to infuse for 5 minutes. Strain the tea into a clean jug and stir in the honey.

2   Leave to cool before chilling. Add lemon juice to taste, and serve poured over ice with a sprig of mint.

celebration lunch

The planning of a summer lunch party is almost as delightful as the meal itself. Picturing the garden filled with handsome men and women clad in those beautiful but impractical clothes beloved by magazine editors, the conversation witty and incisive, the napery starched and the sun shining, is a fond dream of mine. My reality often differs, so I suggest concentrating on simple but delicious food. Stuff that causes comment, but does not leave the hostess flustered. Most of the dishes in this chapter can be started ahead of time, so only a few moments are needed between each course to finish them.

celebration lunch

Serving soup at this meal allows you to manipulate the meal should the weather turn against you. Warm, the soup will cheer; cold, it will refresh. Home-made chicken stock does make a difference, but if time or inclination don't allow for this I use a bottled concentrate called Touch of Taste.

summer soup

2 tablespoons olive oil | **1 large onion, peeled and very finely chopped** | **4 medium main-crop potatoes, peeled and diced (about 500g peeled weight)** | **sea salt and black pepper** | **900ml white chicken stock (see page 159)** | **2 good bunches rocket or watercress, or 2 medium lettuces** | **squeeze of lemon juice (optional)**
To serve **single cream** | **fresh summer herbs**

serves 6

I Heat the oil in a saucepan, and gently fry the onion until softened. Add the potato. Cook for a further 2–3 minutes, then season with salt and pepper and add the stock. Bring to the boil, then simmer until the potato is soft.

2 Now add your chosen green stuff. Cook for 1 minute, then remove from the heat and whizz in batches until smooth. Season to taste, then chill.

3 Before serving, check the seasoning – chilling tends to dull flavours – and add extra salt and pepper if needed. A squeeze of lemon juice will freshen up the soup should it taste a little dull. If the soup seems a little thick, thin it with chilled mineral water.

4 Serve swirled with cream, with a few herbs scattered in each bowl.

Once you've got into the rhythm of bread making, you'll find a dozen different ways to flavour the basic dough. Here I've divided the mix in two to give both an olive bread and a tomato one.

black olive and sun-dried tomato brea

**1 quantity basic bread dough (see page 158) | 110g pitted black olives, chopped | 1 teaspoon chopped coriander |
110g sun-dried tomatoes in oil, drained and chopped**

serves 6

1   Once the bread has risen for the first time (see page 158), knock it back and divide into two pieces. Knead the olives and coriander into one loaf, and the tomatoes into the other.

2   Form each loaf into an oval and place on lined baking sheets. Leave to rise again, for about 40 minutes, or until doubled in size.

3   Preheat the oven to 200°C/400°F/Gas mark 6.

4   Bake in the preheated oven for 20–25 minutes, until golden and hollow-sounding when tapped. Cool on a rack.

The instruction 'peel the eggs' sounds simple, but I know it isn't! Use the end of a tiny coffee spoon, and proceed with care and patience. Making seasoned salts is simple: roast and freshly grind the spice, adding salt to the mix.

quails' eggs with cumin salt

24 fresh quails' eggs | 1 tablespoon cumin seeds (optional) | 2 tablespoons coarse sea salt

serves 6

1   Place the eggs in a saucepan, cover with cold water and bring to the boil. Boil for 4 minutes, then drain and plunge into iced water to cool.

2   To make the cumin salt, dry-fry the cumin seeds in a small pan until they smell nutty. Remove at once and place in a spice grinder or pestle and mortar. Grind until nearly fine, then add the salt and continue to grind until smooth. To serve, peel the eggs and arrange in a dish, with the cumin salt in a small bowl in the centre. Otherwise, simply serve the eggs with plain sea salt. These are good with anchovy biscuits (see page 102).

These are cheats' biscuits, made using ready-made puff pastry. Roll the pastry out as thinly as you can.

anchovy biscuits

225g ready-made puff pastry | I x 50g tin anchovy fillets | 55g Parmesan, freshly grated | chilli flakes (optional)

serves 6

1 Preheat the oven to 200°C/400°F/Gas mark 6.

2 Roll the pastry out as thinly as you can bear. Now mash the anchovies in their oil and spread this over the pastry. Scatter on the cheese and chilli flakes to taste, if using. Roll the pastry up tightly and, starting from the centre and working out, cut into thin medallions.

3 Flatten these lightly with a rolling pin or your hand, and place on baking sheets. Cook in the preheated oven until crisp and golden, about 10 minutes. Cool on a rack.

Keeping things easy is the way to go when preparing a celebration lunch you want to enjoy yourself. This rice dish combines the starchy part of the meal with the vegetables and the sauce, so taking the pressure off the cook.

wild and long-grain rice with summer vegetables

340g mixed wild and long-grain rice | **sea salt and black pepper** | **500g shelled weight fresh peas, baby broad beans or asparagus tips** | **5–20g butter** | **2–3 tablespoons double cream** | **1 tablespoon chopped chervil or tarragon** | **squeeze of lemon juice**

serves 6

1 Place the rice to cook in plenty of boiling salted water, following the packet instructions. Meanwhile, bring a pan of salted water to the boil and cook the chosen vegetable for 2 minutes. Drain and refresh in iced water.

2 Once the rice is bite-tender, drain well. Add the butter and toss. Cover and chill. This can be done up to 4 hours ahead, but no longer.

3 Reheat thoroughly in a microwave for 3–4 minutes at a high heat, tossing well to check all the rice is very hot. Add the cream, chervil or tarragon, and drained peas, beans or asparagus. Taste and adjust seasoning, adding lemon juice to taste.

Baking fish whole is not too alarming an affair, and it does look special. Choose whatever fish is best on the day: bass, mullet, sea trout, monk or a loin of cod would all work well. The fish will take about 25–35 minutes to cook to perfection, so time your meal around this, allowing 5 minutes for the fish to rest once it comes out of the oven.

baked whole fish stuffed with garden herbs

1 x 2kg fresh fish, gutted and scaled | sea salt and black pepper | olive oil | bunch chives | 1 lemon, thinly sliced | good bunch of fresh herbs (fennel, parsley, thyme, tarragon etc.), plus stems | 150ml white wine, plus an equal amount of water

serves 6

1 Clean the fish well, rubbing any blood from the body cavity with salt. Rinse and pat dry. Using a sharp knife, cut deep slashes in the flesh, down to but not through the bone. Do this on both sides of the fish. Drizzle the fish with oil and season well in the slashes. Stuff the fish cavity with chives, lemon slices and herb leaves.

2 Preheat the oven to 200°C/400°F/Gas mark 6.

3 Arrange the herb stems in a line in a baking dish, forming a trivet on which to place the fish. Lay the fish on these, then drizzle over about 2 more tablespoons oil. Pour the wine and water into the pan and, when ready to cook, place in the preheated oven for about 30 minutes, basting at least once. Test the fish to check it is cooked and, if done, remove from the oven and allow to rest for 5 minutes before serving.

If cooking monkfish, ask your fishmonger to remove the central bone, lay the herbs between the fillets, then re-form the fish. You don't need to slash the flesh. Continue as above.

Making your own cheese biscuits might seem a little over the top, but these simple oatcakes are worth the extra effort. With herbs they work well as an accompaniment to cheese, but plain or scented with cinnamon they are delicious for breakfast spread with butter and marmalade. No oatmeal in the house? Simply blitz porridge oats in a food processor fitted with the metal blade until finely chopped!

These delicious oatcakes add a wonderful finishing touch to any meal. They're just as good made with rosemary, sage or even freshly ground cumin. Make round, square or even star-shaped oatcakes.

thyme-scented oatcakes

100g fine oatmeal | ¼ teaspoon fine sea salt | 1 tablespoon fresh thyme leaves, or 1 teaspoon dried | 1 tablespoon fruity olive oil | flour, for dusting | butter, for greasing

serves 6

1 Preheat the oven to 180°C/350°F/Gas mark 4.

2 Pour the oatmeal, salt, thyme and oil into the goblet of a food processor. Whizz until the thyme is chopped and everything is combined. With the motor running, add 4 tablespoons boiling water. The mixture will seem a little wet, so let the motor run for about 1½ minutes and it will all come together. If it seems very dry at this stage, add a dash more water.

3 With your hands, gather the dough up into a ball. While still warm roll out on a floured board, to about 2mm thickness. Cut out your oatcakes and place on a greased baking sheet. Bake in the preheated oven for about 15 minutes, or until lightly coloured.

4 The oatcakes will crisp on cooling. Store in an airtight tin and serve with cheese.

This parfait can be served with a fruit compote prepared in the same way as the fruits for the summer puddings (see over).

poppy-seed parfait

4 large egg yolks | **1 tablespoon runny honey** | **110g caster sugar** | **225ml milk** | **1 vanilla pod** | **400ml double cream** | **55g poppy seeds**

serves 6

1 Start by placing the egg yolks, honey and sugar in a heavy-bottomed pan and whisking them with a balloon whisk. Place the pan over a very low heat, and continue to whisk while the mixture is warm. The eggs should fluff up, double in volume and become very thick.

2 In a separate pan, bring the milk and vanilla to the boil, then strain into the hot sabayon, whisking constantly. Leave to cool.

3 Whip the cream until it holds soft peaks, then fold in the sabayon and the poppy seeds. Spoon into a clingfilm-lined loaf tin, and freeze.

4 Serve cut into slices with some red fruit and crisp cardamom biscuits (see page 19).

Whilst these individual sponge puddings are best eaten the day they are made, they can be gently warmed through if made a day ahead.

almond sponge summer puddings

110g soft butter, plus extra for greasing | 110g plain flour, plus extra for dusting | 1 teaspoon baking powder | 110g caster sugar | 2 large eggs, beaten | finely grated rind of 1 lemon | 55g ground almonds | 110g each of redcurrants and blackcurrants | 150ml red wine | caster sugar to taste | 2 tablespoons crème de cassis | 250g raspberries | 250g small strawberries, hulled | whipped cream and icing sugar

serves 6

1   Butter and flour six small ramekin dishes, and place these on a baking sheet. Preheat the oven to 180°C/350°F/Gas mark 4.

2   Sift the flour with the baking powder. Cream the butter and sugar together until light. Add the egg, then the flour, lemon rind and ground almonds. Mix well.

3   Divide the mixture between the prepared dishes, and bake in the preheated oven for 15–20 minutes, or until well risen, golden brown and pulling away from the sides of the ramekins. Allow to sit for 5 minutes before turning out and placing in a large dish.

4   Place the stringed currants and the wine in a small pan along with 2–3 tablespoons caster sugar. Warm until the fruit gives up its juice and the sugar dissolves. Stir in the cassis, then add the remaining berries and cook for 1–2 minutes. Strain the fruit from the syrup, reserving both.

5   Spoon the syrup from the fruit over the cakes, and allow the cakes to soak this up. The puddings can be made ahead up to this point.

6   To serve, warm the sponges in a low oven (140°C/275°F/Gas mark 1), then place on a plate. Spoon over the fruit, then top with whipped cream and a dusting of icing sugar.

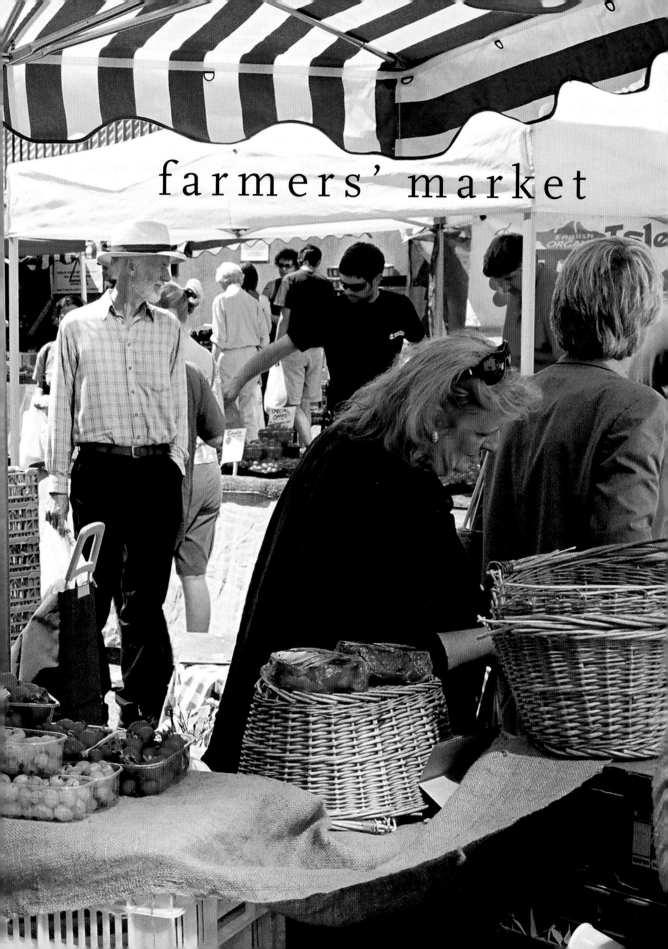

farmers' market

Farmers' markets have been one of the great incentives that have helped encourage folk to eat good, home-grown and locally produced foods. They have really taken off, and can even be found in towns and cities where the old-fashioned street markets have ceased to trade. The delight of market shopping is one of the things we most like about foreign holidays. How much more pleasure, then, to be able to buy wonderful fresh food direct from the man or woman responsible for it, here at home. One word of caution: don't leave your scepticism completely at home; you do occasionally find rogue traders even at farmers' markets. Being intensely seasonal, farmers' markets perfectly mirror exactly what is freshest and best, so be guided by what you find offered for sale, rather than a recipe, when shopping at one.

farmers' market

You nearly always find fish stalls at farmers' markets – I'm not sure why, as they never sell farmed fish. Local smoke-houses will smoke haddock or cod in the old-fashioned way, with never a hint of the spray tan that affects mass-produced smoked fish. This soup can be made – up to the point where the fish is returned to the pan – a day ahead. When needed, simply reheat the soup, drop in the fish and continue from there.

haddock, potato and corn chowder

450g smoked haddock | **1–2 fresh corn cobs, when available** | **2 tablespoons light olive oil** | **30g butter** | **2 onions, peeled and finely chopped** | **2 leeks, halved lengthwise and thinly sliced** | **3 ribs celery, thinly sliced** | **4 medium potatoes, peeled and diced** | **2 teaspoons chopped fresh thyme or ½ teaspoon dried** | **150ml double cream** | **Tabasco sauce** | **sea salt and black pepper** | **handful of freshly chopped parsley**

serves 4–6

I Place the smoked haddock in a pan and cover with 900ml cold water. Bring this to the boil, then remove from the heat. Allow the fish to sit in the hot water for about 10 minutes before removing it. Reserve the cooking water to use as stock. Break the fish into biggish flakes, removing all skin and bone.

2 Using a sharp knife, cut the kernels from the corn cobs.

3 Heat the oil and butter in a deep pan. Add the onion, corn, leek, celery and potato, and fry for a few minutes until starting to soften. Stir in the thyme, followed by the smoked haddock stock, and bring to the boil. Reduce the heat to a simmer, and cook for 10 minutes until the vegetables have cooked through.

4 With a potato masher, lightly mash the vegetables to break up the potato and give a rough texture. Add the cream and smoked haddock to the soup, and season with a good shake of Tabasco and some black pepper. You may need to add salt at this stage.

5 Bring back to the boil and cook for about a minute, then stir in the parsley and serve.

This is a good place for my rant about buying cheap chicken. You must never do it. It's very simple: mass production in the chicken industry is one of the areas of food production that has me wincing. Do treat all meat and fish as something special, and pay the price for it. Delicious food, with no qualms of conscience.

pan-roast chicken breast with roasted cherry tomatoes and bread sauce

4 medium free-range chicken breasts, with the skin on but fully boned | **sea salt and black pepper**

For the tomatoes **225g cherry tomatoes** | **2–3 tablespoons olive oil** | **I teaspoon chopped thyme leaves** | **sea salt and black pepper** | **crushed dried chilli to taste**

For the bread sauce **600ml milk** | **55g butter** | **I onion, peeled and studded with cloves** | **I bay leaf** | **3 sprigs thyme** | **115g white breadcrumbs** | **sea salt and black pepper** | **4 tablespoons single cream**

serves 4

I   For the bread sauce, place the milk, butter, clove-studded onion and herbs in a pan. Bring up to the boil, then remove and leave for 20 minutes. Preheat the oven to 200°C/400°F/Gas mark 6. Strain and return the flavoured milk to the pan, discarding the solids. Stir in the breadcrumbs and simmer, stirring often, for 4 minutes. Season and stir in the cream.

2   Place the tomatoes, oil and thyme in an ovenproof dish and season to taste, adding some chilli flakes for extra kick. Roast in the preheated oven for 15–20 minutes.

3   Heat a heavy-bottomed frying pan until very hot. Put the chicken breasts into the pan skin-side down, turn the heat down to low-to-medium, and do not touch the chicken for 10 minutes, or until you can see that the meat is nearly cooked through.

4   Season the uncooked side of the chicken then turn the breast over and cook the underside for about 5–6 minutes. Remove from the heat and allow to sit for 5 minutes – make sure the chicken is cooked through. Carve the chicken breasts into slices and arrange each portion on a couple of spoonfuls of bread sauce with the roasted tomatoes on the side. A delicious gravy can be made by adding some fresh chicken stock to the pan juices and bubbling to reduce.

Well-hung beef is the secret of this dish. Farmers' markets are a good source, as you can talk to the producer about the breed and cut of the meat, and discuss how long the meat has been hung. Rump, sirloin and fillet are all delicious, but other cuts such as flank can be both tender and tasty. Remember to use your eyes when cooking steak: look to see how far the heat has penetrated before turning the meat.

grilled steak with red onion and herb salad

4 x 170–225g steak, ideally cut no less than 2cm thick | **olive oil** | **1–2 tablespoons black peppercorns, crushed** | **sea salt**

For the salad **2 medium red onions, peeled and thinly sliced** | **2 tablespoons tarragon vinegar** | **2 handfuls fresh watercress, rocket or other spicy salad leaves** | **good handful of parsley leaves** | **6 tablespoons olive oil** | **1 teaspoon runny honey** | **sea salt and black pepper**

serves 4

1. Brush the steaks lightly with olive oil and liberally coat with crushed peppercorns. Allow the steaks to sit for about 10–15 minutes, or longer is fine if you have the time.

2. Meanwhile, heat a heavy-bottomed dry frying pan for at least 10 minutes over a high heat. Place the onion in the tarragon vinegar and leave this to one side for 10 minutes.

3. Just before cooking, sprinkle the steaks with a little salt. Place in the pan and DO NOT TOUCH for about 4 minutes. Turn and cook the other side for about 3–4 minutes. Now test the steak to see if it is cooked to your liking. I use a cold skewer inserted into the centre of the meat. If it feels cold against your lip when you pull it out after 10 seconds, the meat is blue; if warm, pink; if hot, well done. This technique will mean your steak has a lovely crusty outside and juicy middle. Remember, the more you fuss over food, the more it misbehaves.

4. To make the salad, drain the onion, reserving the vinegar, and toss the onion with the salad and herb leaves. Mix the reserved vinegar with the oil, honey and seasoning to make a sharpish, sweetish dressing. Just before serving, toss through the onion salad and serve.

One of the joys of farmers' markets is that you can buy real sausages. I like to make individual toads (or should that be holes?), but this recipe works well cooked in one large dish (about a 1.2-litre oven dish), if you don't have the requisite Yorkshire pudding tins.

toad in the hole

2 large eggs | 100ml milk | 125g plain flour | 1 tablespoon finely chopped sage | sea salt and black pepper |
4 teaspoons olive oil | 8 sausages
For the onion gravy **2 red onions, peeled and thinly sliced | 2 tablespoons olive oil | 1 tablespoon plain flour**
300ml chicken stock (see page 159) | sea salt and black pepper | Worcestershire sauce to taste

serves 4

1 Preheat the oven to 200°C/400°F/Gas mark 6.

2 Whisk the eggs, milk, flour, sage and 50ml water together, adding a pinch each of salt and pepper, and allow to stand for a few minutes.

3 Put a teaspoon of oil into each of four individual batter pudding dishes, then add two sausages to each one. Bake in the preheated oven for about 5 minutes.

4 Remove and turn the sausages over. Pour a quarter of the batter into each dish and return to the oven for a further 20 minutes, or until the puddings are well risen and crispy brown.

5 Meanwhile, make the onion gravy. Fry the onion in a pan with the oil over a low heat until it has softened. Turn up the heat and cook until the onion is a deep brown. Stir in the flour, then add the stock, stirring well. Simmer for about 5 minutes, adding more liquid if needed. Season to taste with salt, pepper and Worcestershire sauce.

6 Serve the toads with a little gravy alongside, with a green vegetable – whatever is in season.

Most farmers' markets have wonderful bread. This recipe is called many things: 'pain perdu' in France, 'French toast' in the United States, but here I think 'eggy bread' works well. It can be a savoury dish served with some good dry-cure Suffolk bacon, or a dessert when served with runny jam or crushed fruit. I often eat it for an indulgent Sunday breakfast.

eggy bread with jersey cream and crushed fruit

2 large eggs, beaten | **150ml creamy milk** | **4 x 1cm slices good white bread or brioche (raisin bread works well, too)** | **butter, for frying**

To serve **500g mixed berries** | **2–4 tablespoons caster sugar** | **loads of thick Jersey cream**

serves 4

I   Whisk the eggs and milk together, and pour into a shallow dish. Lay in the bread slices, and allow them to absorb as much of the mixture as possible, turning once or twice. They will need to soak for about 4–5 minutes.

2   Heat a frying pan to medium hot and put in a generous knob of butter. Lift the bread from the egg mix and lay the slices in the pan. They should not touch, so it may be necessary to fry in batches. Cook over a moderate heat for about 3–4 minutes, or until the underside is golden. Turn and cook the other side until it is also golden. Keep warm while you cook the other pieces.

3   If frying in batches, wipe the pan with kitchen roll before continuing cooking. The first lot of butter will have burnt a little and can give a bitter flavour to the subsequent slices.

4   While the bread is frying, place the berries and about 2 tablespoons of caster sugar in a bowl and crush them lightly with a fork. Add more sugar if necessary. You can add a little cassis if you have some around. Spoon the fruit over the eggy bread and pour over some rich yellow Jersey cream. Serve at once.

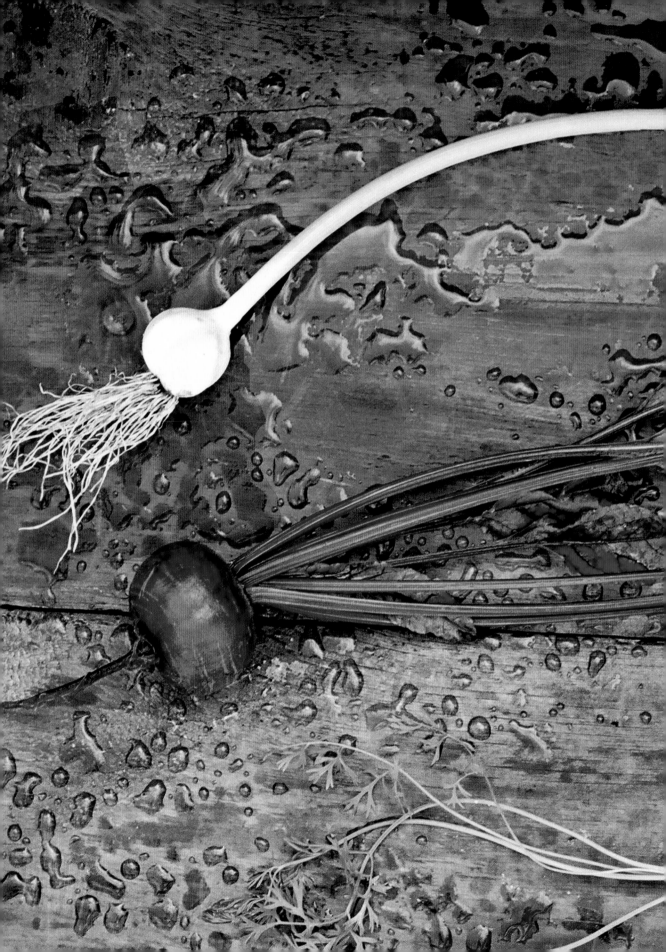

allotment
harvest supper

Since living in the country, I've longed for an allotment. The waiting list stands in my way, but it is my husband's dogged refusal to dig any allotment of mine that will finally stop me from fulfilling this dream. I feel that I'm more of a planter-gatherer than a digger, and standing rain-drenched in the mud, spade in hand, doesn't fit with the romantic image I have. Not everyone is as lightweight as me, and so allotments are regaining their popularity and understandably so. Growing your own vegetables is as much of a delight as eating them – garden fresh, sweet and delicious. The true flavours of the seasons are clear, and even the least green-thumbed of us can reap successful harvests with today's top-class seeds and advice. As the summer draws to a close, a celebration of the garden's bounty should include meat and fish as free-range as the vegetables that will accompany them.

allotment harvest supper

Belly pork is if anything these days a little too lean, so ask your butcher for pork from one of the many rare-breed pigs now being farmed. The joint will need long, slow cooking to render the tougher fibres meltingly tender, then a quick flash under the grill to crisp up the crackling.

roast belly of pork with roast fruit

1kg belly pork, rind on and bone in | **6–8 sage leaves** | **6–8 thin strips lemon zest** | **olive oil** | **sea salt and black pepper** | **3 each of firm apples, quinces and pears** | **2 medium onions, quartered, skin on** | **600ml chicken stock (see page 159)**

serves 6

1 Preheat the oven to 180°C/350°F/Gas mark 4.

2 Ask the butcher to score the skin of the pork, or do this yourself using a Stanley knife. For crisp crackling, cut the score marks close together. Take the sage leaves and strips of lemon zest, and press these into the fat between the score marks. Rub the joint all over with oil and season with salt and pepper.

3 Place the joint in a shallow covered casserole or baking tin, and arrange the fruit and onion around the meat. I leave the fruit whole, core in, as they look most attractive this way.

4 Roast the pork in the preheated oven for 2 hours, basting both meat and fruit from time to time. It may be necessary to hook out some of the apples if they seem to be cooked. Once the pork is cooked through and tender, remove the dish from the oven.

5 Heat the grill. Carefully spoon the fruit and onion on to a serving dish. Place the pork on the grill pan. Tip off most of the fat from the roasting tin and pour in the stock. Stir until the gravy boils, then simmer to reduce. Strain and adjust seasoning.

6 Place the pork under the grill and watch carefully. Grill until the skin bubbles and crisps. Serve with the roast fruit and onion-flavoured gravy.

Before you gasp in horror that I'm using cod, let me explain that off the shores of Suffolk cod are line-caught throughout the winter and spring. I buy cod freshly landed on the beach. Cod is still widely available in fish shops, but like all wild food we must be prepared to pay a good price. Try home salting it, and using the fish for fish cakes or brandade. Vary the salting times to suit your recipe: salting cod really transforms it. This is a wonderful recipe. There needs to be a little forward planning, as ideally the cod, usually a rather wet fish, should be salted for 6 hours, but the improved texture and flavour is worth a little effort. The barley part of this recipe is not really a risotto, but cooked in a style to resemble risotto. Thick, rich mascarpone cheese is stirred into the barley to give the creamy texture necessary for risotto.

salt cod with barley 'risotto'

6 thick slices fresh cod, skin on, about 170g each (cut from the thick end of the fillet) | 3 tablespoons Maldon salt flakes or coarse rock salt | finely grated zest of 1 lemon | olive oil, for frying
For the barley 'risotto' 3 tablespoons each of chopped shallot, celery, carrot and leek | 2 tablespoons olive oil | 225g barley, washed | 750ml chicken or vegetable stock (see page 159) | sea salt and black pepper | 2–3 tablespoons mascarpone | 2–3 tablespoons freshly grated Parmesan

serves 4

I   Wash and trim the cod fillets as necessary. Feeling carefully with your fingers, locate and remove the pin bones from the centre of the fillets. Lay the fish, skin-side down, in a shallow glass or ceramic dish and, having mixed the salt with the lemon zest, sprinkle this mixture evenly over the fillets. Cover the dish with clingfilm and leave in a cool place or the bottom of the refrigerator for 6 hours.

2   About half an hour before you want to serve, start the 'risotto' (although, unlike rice risotto, this dish is very well tempered and will sit happily for a good half hour – add a little extra stock and reheat gently before serving). Gently fry the vegetables in the olive oil for about 3–4 minutes until soft. Now add the barley and fry for a further few minutes. Add half of the stock and simmer over a low heat, stirring often, for about 20 minutes. As the risotto dries out, add more stock, a ladleful at a time.

3 Taste the barley and, when tender, stop adding the stock and stir in salt and pepper to taste, along with the mascarpone and Parmesan.

4 Wash the salted cod fillets well under running cold water, then pat them completely dry using kitchen paper. Heat a heavy-bottomed frying pan until hot. Smear the fish with olive oil, then place the fillets in the pan and leave to cook for 4–5 minutes, or until well coloured. Turn and cook the other side, also for about 4 minutes. Allow the fish to rest in a warm place for about 5 minutes before serving on a bed of barley risotto.

Look for freshly dug beetroots for this recipe. A bonus of buying beets resplendent with foliage is that the leaves – or beet greens, as they are known – make a delicious vegetable.

beets with orange and chive dressing

12 or so small beetroots

For the dressing **juice and finely grated zest of 1 orange | squeeze of lemon juice | ¼ teaspoon clear honey | 50ml olive oil | 2 tablespoons snipped chives | sea salt and black pepper**

serves 4

I   Wash the beets well and place in a pan. Cover with cold water and bring to the boil. Simmer for 15–25 minutes, depending on size. The beets are ready when tender if pierced with a skewer. Drain and allow to cool. Once cold, slip off the skins, roots etc., and either cut into quarters or leave whole. Arrange in a shallow serving dish.

2   Mix the dressing ingredients together, taste and correct seasoning. Pour the dressing over the beets and serve.

These sweet carrots are excellent with roast pork or chicken, but not, I think, with beef.

honey dill carrots

450g organic carrots | 300ml chicken or vegetable stock (see page 159) | 30g butter | 1 tablespoon honey | 1 tablespoon chopped dill | sea salt and black pepper

serves 4

I   Peel the carrots and cut into discs (baby carrots can be cooked whole). Cook in the stock until just tender, then turn up the heat to evaporate all but 1 tablespoon of the liquid.

2   Mix in the butter and honey, and cook for a further 2–3 minutes over a low heat. Stir in the dill, correct the seasoning and serve.

Peel the roasted garlic cloves to reveal a thick caramelised purée, which is delicious mashed and eaten with these sweet-tasting new potatoes.

olive-oil roast new potatoes with garli

675g new potatoes, scrubbed | **few sprigs of rosemary** | **I pink garlic bulb or 10–15 pink garlic cloves, unpeeled** | **4–6 tablespoons olive oil** | **sea salt and black pepper**

serves 4

I   Preheat the oven to 200°C/400°F/Gas mark 6.

2   Dry the scrubbed potatoes, then place in a roasting dish along with the rosemary and garlic cloves. Drizzle over the oil, shaking the dish to make sure all the potatoes are coated. Season well with salt and pepper, then roast in the preheated oven for 30–40 minutes, or until golden and tender.

Simple, old-fashioned and delicious fruit crumbles are always welcome. I always leave the stones in the plums. I'm sure it makes no difference to the flavour, but it would be tragic to miss the chance of playing 'Tinker, Tailor, Soldier, Sailor'.

plum crumble

1kg plums (any sort will be fine) | **2 tablespoons caster sugar** | **I teaspoon freshly ground cinnamon** |
butter, for greasing
For the crumble topping **55g blanched almonds** | **55g rolled oats** | **170g butter** | **170g plain flour** |
I teaspoon freshly ground cinnamon

serves 6

I   Preheat the oven to 180°C/350°F/Gas mark 4.

2   Cut the plums in half, leaving in the stones. Mix the sugar and cinnamon together, and toss the fruit in this. Place in a buttered ovenproof dish, and bake in the preheated oven for 10 minutes. Gently toss the fruit to mix.

3   Meanwhile, whizz the crumble ingredients together in a food processor, so that the oats and nuts are lightly chopped. Scatter this topping over the fruit, and continue to bake until the fruit is bubbling and the crumble crisp, about 25 minutes. Serve hot or warm with thick cream.

preserving bee

In the same way that I am incapable of walking past a field of strawberries without thinking of jam, I find the first signs of autumn have me rushing for my preserving pan. Whilst making jams and jellies might seem a little old-fashioned, there are few delights to rival the thrill of seeing jars of jewel-bright preserves on your pantry shelf. Should you feel anxious about jam-making, begin with pickles. Whatever you decide, be choosy and use only fruit and vegetables in good condition. Use freshly ground whole spices and good wine, cider or distilled malt vinegar for pickles. White sugar is best for jams and jellies, but the flavour of raw muscovado sugar is wonderful in chutneys. Always use glass or china dishes for brining and stainless steel or enamelled cast-iron for cooking. Pot into spotlessly clean jars and top with vinegar-proof seals. Store preserves in a cool, dry place away from the light.

preserving bee

A friend of mine grows chillies by the score in his greenhouse. This 'jam' is a way of preserving both their flavour and their heat. Chillies can be dried very successfully if spread out well and left in a warm place.

smoked red pepper and chilli jam

5 large red peppers | **4–8 hot chilli peppers** | **2 teaspoons smoked Spanish paprika** | **350ml wine vinegar** | **1.3kg preserving sugar** | **1 bottle Certo (fruit pectin)** | **Tabasco sauce to taste**

makes 4 medium jars

1   Cut the peppers and chillies in half, and remove all the seeds and stalks. Place the flesh in a blender or food processor, and chop finely.

2   Put the pepper mixture into a deep heavy saucepan and add the paprika, vinegar and sugar. Place over a moderate heat and bring the mixture slowly to the boil, stirring, until the sugar has dissolved. Boil rapidly for 5 minutes.

3   Remove from the heat, stir in the Certo and taste, adding Tabasco until the mixture is hot enough for you. Remember that the jelly will taste less hot when cold.

4   Return the pan to the heat, and bring back to the boil. Cook at a full rolling boil for 2 minutes, then allow it to settle for about 5 minutes before potting into sterilised jars.

We can welcome a glut of apples because they form the base for so many preserves. I flavour jellies with flowers and exotic spices - make other flavoured jellies in the same way as below using chillies, lemongrass, rosemary etc. to scent them - but a simple apple or crab-apple jelly is perfect on buttered toast for breakfast.

lavender jelly

2kg cooking apples, washed and chopped | 3 tablespoons lavender flowers | few blackberries | white sugar (see below)

makes about 6–8 small jars

I   Put the apples into a large preserving pan with 2 tablespoons of the lavender flowers and the blackberries. Add 1.5 litres water and simmer until the apples are very soft.

2   Spoon the contents of the pan into a jelly bag set over a bowl, and allow to drip overnight.

3   Measure the resulting liquid and allow 500g sugar for each 500ml. Place the apple liquid, sugar and the remaining lavender flowers into a clean preserving pan, and stir over a low heat until the sugar has dissolved. Now turn up the heat and bring the mixture to a full rolling boil. Cook until setting point is reached, then pot into small jars.

Ketchup doesn't need to be made with tomatoes; I always make mine with plums. It simply demands plump pork sausages and mashed potato or, better yet, egg and chips.

spicy fruit ketchup

2kg plums | 170g chopped dates | 110g raisins | 1 large onion, peeled and chopped, | 4 plump garlic cloves, peeled | 55g fresh root ginger, peeled and grated | 1 tablespoon coriander seeds, freshly ground | 1 teaspoon allspice berries, freshly ground | good pinch of cayenne pepper | 55g salt | 1 litre malt or wine vinegar | 300g light muscovado sugar | 1 tablespoon turmeric | ½ nutmeg, freshly grated

makes about 2kg

1 Wash and stone the plums and place in a large pan with the dates, raisins, onion, garlic and ginger. Now add the coriander, allspice, cayenne and salt, pour over 500ml of the vinegar and bring to the boil. Simmer for about 30–40 minutes, or until the fruit is very soft. Allow to cool before rubbing through a mouli or sieving. Place the purée back into the washed pan, and add the remaining vinegar, sugar, turmeric and nutmeg. Bring the mixture to the boil. Simmer for 30 minutes, stirring often, then cool and pour into clean bottles or jars. Store for at least a month before use.

Home-made fruit vinegars are a cinch to prepare and give both colour and flavour to salads and cooked food. Try using raspberry or blackberry vinegar with duck. Delicious.

raspberry and other fruit vinegars

250g fresh or frozen blackberries, raspberries or blackcurrants | 55g caster sugar | 400ml white wine vinegar

makes about 500ml

1 Warm the fruit and sugar together until the juices run and the sugar has dissolved. Scrape the mixture into a clean glass jug or bowl, and add the vinegar. Cover with clingfilm and leave for at least one week, but better for three weeks. Strain the vinegar into a clean bottle.

Apple butter is really a long simmered purée that slices like quince cheese, or membrillo, and like membrillo, apple butter is wonderful with mature Cheddar.

apple butter

1.8kg apples, peeled, cored and chopped | 6 cloves, crushed | ½ nutmeg, crushed | 10cm cinnamon stick, crushed | 5cm piece of fresh root ginger, crushed | 1.3kg white sugar

makes about 3kg

1 Cook the fruit in 500ml water until you have a thick purée. Meanwhile, wrap all the spices loosely in a muslin bag and add to the apple along with the sugar, and stir well, mixing until the sugar has dissolved. Simmer over a very low heat for about 2 hours. The purée will become very thick and dark. If necessary, place the pan on a heat diffuser to prevent from sticking and burning.

2 To test that the 'butter' is ready, allow a spoonful to cool on a chilled tea plate: it should hold its shape on the plate. Pot the butter into sterilised jars and cover in the usual manner.

I was, one year, very successful growing tiny pickling onions in my garden. More usually I use small shallots for this recipe.

sweet chilli-pickled shallots

1kg shallots | 225g salt | about 1 litre distilled vinegar | about 3 tablespoons raw muscovado sugar | 2–4 bay leaves | 2–4 dried chillies, crushed | 1 plump fresh garlic bulb, broken into cloves and peeled

makes 6 medium jars

1 Peel the shallots and place them in a brine made by dissolving the salt in 1.2 litres water. Leave overnight. Meanwhile, heat the vinegar with the sugar, bay leaves and chillies. When hot, turn off the heat and allow the vinegar to infuse overnight as well.

2 The next day wash and dry the shallots. Pack them into clean jars, with the garlic, and pour over the vinegar, pressing the shallots down well. Cover and leave for two months.

This lovely recipe comes from my mother, and is a good way of using windfall apples. It has the particular appeal of combining ease of preparation and economy with flavour. Store for about a month before using with grilled cheese, sausages or just about anything.

easy apple and onion chutney

about 2kg cooking apples | 900g onions, peeled and finely chopped | 55g garlic, peeled and chopped | 55g fresh root ginger, peeled and chopped | 1–2 large fresh red chillies, seeded and chopped | 1 litre distilled vinegar | 560g light muscovado sugar | 2 tablespoons ground turmeric | 1 tablespoon salt

makes about 6–8 medium jars

1 Cut away any bad spots from the apples, then peel and core them to give you about 1.8kg in weight. Using a food processor or sharp knife, finely chop the fruit, then place in a large pan. Add the onion, garlic, ginger and chilli. Pour in the vinegar and stir in the sugar, turmeric and salt.

2 Bring the mixture to the boil, stirring until the sugar has dissolved, then simmer until thick, about 1 hour. Stir often as the mixture reduces, to avoid it catching on the bottom of the pan and burning.

3 Spoon the hot pickle into spotlessly clean jars, and top each one with a lid that has a vinegar-proof seal.

The lovely thing about this mustard pickle is that unlike most chutney or pickles you can eat it the day after it's made or even the same evening if needs must! Don't omit the salting stage: this is necessary to remove excess water from the vegetables which, if not leeched out, would dilute the vinegar. The upshot of this would be spoilt pickles, not something to contemplate.

piccalilli

1 medium cauliflower | **450g pickling onions** | **2 ridged cucumbers or courgettes** | **225g runner beans** | **2 bulbs of plump garlic cloves** | **225g salt**
For the sauce **30g plain flour** | **225g white sugar** | **1 tablespoon ground turmeric** | **55g mustard powder** | **700ml distilled vinegar**

makes 1kg, or 6 medium jars

1 Prepare the vegetables first. Separate the florets of the cauliflower; peel the onions and leave whole; dice the cucumbers or courgettes; slice the beans into 2.5cm pieces; and peel the garlic cloves, leaving them whole. Put all these into a brine made with the salt and 1 litre water, and leave overnight. Rinse and drain well.

2 Make the sauce by mixing the flour, sugar, turmeric and mustard, and adding enough vinegar to make a paste. Now mix in the remaining vinegar and pour into a saucepan. Bring to the boil, whisking constantly, to give a smooth, thick sauce. Simmer for 4–5 minutes.

3 Add the vegetables to the sauce, bring back to the boil and simmer for about 3 minutes. Put into spotlessly clean jars, and top with a lid that has a vinegar-proof seal.

Picking berries from a late summer garden can yield a surprising number of varieties perfect for pots of dark-hued 'jumbleberry' jam.

jumbleberry jam

You will need an equal weight of berries and sugar for this recipe, and for each 500g of fruit you will need the juice of 1 large lemon

1   Mix the berries and sugar together in a preserving pan, and squeeze in the lemon juice. Stirring gently, warm the mixture until the sugar dissolves. Turn up the heat and bring to the boil. Cook at a full rolling boil until the jam tests positive for a set (see page 143).

2   Spoon into sterilised jars, top with seals and label.

Use this recipe as a base for fruit chutneys. I replace the peaches with mangoes if I find them at the right price, up the amount of chilli and add about 1 tablespoon of crushed coriander seeds - and you have a perfect chutney to serve with curries.

peach and ginger chutney

1.5kg ripe peaches | 2 large onions, peeled | 500g mixed dried fruit (dates, raisins, apricots) | 6 plump garlic cloves, peeled | 1 x 5cm piece fresh root ginger | 2–4 dried chillies, crushed | 1 litre cider vinegar | 675g light muscovado sugar

makes 6 medium jars

1 Dip the peaches in boiling water, then slip off the skins. Chop the fruit, discarding the stones. Chop the onions, and put these along with the dried fruit, the garlic and peaches into a preserving pan. Grate in the ginger root, then add the crushed chillies and cider vinegar. Stir in the sugar and place over a low heat.

2 Bring slowly to boiling point, stirring from time to time. Once the sugar has dissolved, turn up the heat and allow the chutney to bubble until thick. Stir often while the chutney cooks, and keep checking that the chutney at the bottom of the pan has not caught and burnt.

3 Pot into sterilised jars and cover with vinegar-proof seals.

additional tips

If it's necessary to wash the fruit before cooking, do drain it well on a clean tea towel.

You will need a large, shallow pan for cooking your preserves. The surface area must be wide to help with the evaporation needed to reach a set, and the pan must be deep enough for you to cook at a full rolling boil, i.e. a boil that cannot be stirred down.

Before you begin, stack some saucers in the freezer for use in the wrinkle test for setting.

Run your jars through a hot wash in your dishwasher, and keep them warm in a warming drawer or low oven ready for potting.

Make sure you have plenty of cellophane seals, or save the lids from the jars and reuse.

Don't double up quantities given in a recipe; you need plenty of space in your pan.

Boil your jams or jellies for about 5 minutes after the sugar has dissolved. Then test for a set (see below). Always take the pan off the heat while you are doing so. If not ready, boil for another 2–3 minutes, then test again.

To test for a set, spoon a little jam or jelly on to a chilled tea saucer and leave to cool. If the surface wrinkles when lightly pushed with a fingertip, the preserve is ready to pot. Always take the pan from the heat while you test, returning the mixture to a full boil and continuing to cook if setting point has not been reached.

And do label your jars! You may think you'll remember what is in each one, but you won't, and it can be embarrassing serving chilli jam for breakfast.

One perfect way to prolong the warmth and sweetness of summer is to make these aromatic sugars. Most of us have a jar of vanilla sugar on the shelf and to these we can add lavender, lemon verbena, rose and thyme. Rosemary and bay work well too.

flower-flavoured sugars

250g caster sugar | good handful of lavender flowers

makes 250g   I   Mix the sugar and dry flowers in a container with a lid, and leave for three weeks.

Home-made drinks that mimic French cordials are simple to put together. I make cassis, and raspberry and blackberry vodka in the summer, and cranberry vodka in the winter. Use supermarket brand spirits and really fresh ripe fruit.

raspberry or blackberry gin or vodka

450g raspberries or blackberries | 225g caster sugar | 750ml gin or vodka

makes I litre   I   Warm the fruit and sugar together until the juices of the fruit begin to run. Scrape into a bowl or jug, and pour over the gin or vodka. Stir and cover with clingfilm, sealing tightly.

2   Stir daily for four to five days, then strain into bottles (the original gin or vodka ones are best) and seal.

These drinks are best left for about four weeks before drinking, either as a liqueur or diluted with white wine. Fruit-flavoured vodkas can be stored in the freezer once maturation has taken place.

end of summer lunch

Well, summer is nearly over, but there is just enough time and good weather for a few final garden lunches. These to my mind are some of the best summer meals. Replete with good food and part of enjoying an Indian summer, meals late in the season allow time for contemplation and reflection.

But no time for maudlin thoughts. After all, summer may be over, but autumn and winter, wood smoke and crumpets, all beckon ... Life is good.

end-of-summer lunch

Baking powder breads are quick to make and endlessly variable. I love the taste of fresh corn, but thawed frozen corn kernels can be used instead.

sweetcorn, cheddar and onion muffins

I large red onion, peeled and sliced | 4 tablespoons olive oil | 225g plain flour | 55g instant polenta |
I tablespoon baking powder | I teaspoon salt | 2 medium eggs | 200ml buttermilk, or milk with a squeeze of
lemon juice | I fresh red chilli, seeded and chopped (optional) | 225g sweetcorn kernels, cut from about 3 cobs |
85g Cheddar or Parmesan, grated

makes 12

1 Preheat the oven to 200°C/400°F/Gas mark 6.

2 Fry the onion in half the olive oil until soft and
brown. Sift the flour, polenta, baking powder and
salt together into a bowl. Beat the eggs with the
buttermilk and remaining oil. Mix this into the flour,
along with all the remaining ingredients, apart from
30g of the cheese, scraping any oil from the pan
into the bowl.

3 Spoon the mixture into 12 paper-lined muffin cups
and top with the reserved cheese. Bake in the
preheated oven for 20 minutes, or until well risen
and golden brown. Cool on a rack before serving.

Swiss chard is best picked quite young before the stems toughen and become fibrous. Spinach would make an acceptable alternative.

swiss chard and gruyère quiche

180g home-made shortcrust pastry (see page 158) or a packet of bought pastry

For the filling **good bunch of Swiss chard | sea salt and black pepper | 1 medium onion, peeled and chopped | 1 garlic clove, peeled and chopped | 2 tablespoons olive oil | 6 large eggs | 300ml double cream | 110g Gruyère cheese, grated | handful of chervil, chopped**

serves 8

1 Start by making the pastry. Chill for 30 minutes, then roll out and use to line a deep 23cm flan tin.

2 Preheat the oven to 200°C/400°F/Gas mark 6.

3 Slice the chard leaves and stems, and blanch in boiling salted water for 1 minute. Drain and press out as much liquid as possible. This is important, so be vigilant. Cook the onion and garlic in the olive oil until soft and beginning to colour. Beat the eggs with the cream, and season well.

4 Mix the cooled onion mixture, cheese, chervil and chard into the custard, and pour into the prepared pastry case. Bake in the preheated oven for 40–50 minutes. Serve hot or cold.

Cooking lamb in big chunks is an idea I've borrowed from Greece. Shoulder is the best cut, and you will have to explain to your butcher that you want the meat cut through the bone into 7.5cm cubes, i.e. individual servings. These are then cooked in a covered casserole for about 2 hours, after which time the lid is removed and the meat cooked until golden brown and meltingly tender.

baked lamb

**1 large shoulder of lamb, cut into large 7.5cm cubes | olive oil | sea salt and black pepper |
2 whole garlic bulbs | 4–6 sprigs rosemary**

serves 6

1 Preheat the oven to 160°C/325°F/Gas mark 3.

2 Wash and dry the lamb, then rub the chunks all over with oil and season well with salt and pepper. Place in a shallow lidded casserole dish. Cut the garlic bulbs in half through the equator and tuck them, along with the rosemary, among the lamb chunks.

3 Put on the lid and place in the preheated oven for 2 hours. Now remove the lid and continue to cook the lamb until it is well browned and the skin crispy.

4 Lift the meat out of the casserole, and serve with the roasted garlic and fresh mint sauce (see opposite).

Mint grows like a weed and so can be on hand, fresh cut, in even the smallest of gardens. There are dozens of varieties, so grow several. I prefer a traditional garden mint for this sauce, but often mix in another variety to tweak the flavour a little. Make the sauce about an hour before you need it.

real mint sauce

good bunch of mint | **about 2–3 tablespoons caster sugar** | **1 tablespoon wine vinegar**

serves 6

1 Pick the leaves from the coarser stems. You now need to chop the mint finely. I find chopping in a food processor best, as the mint maintains its colour better if a little of the vinegar is added at the beginning. Place the leaves and thin stems in a food processor bowl, add a little of the sugar and vinegar, and whizz the leaves until they are finely chopped.

2 Scrape the mix from the goblet into a pretty bowl and add vinegar and sugar until the sauce suits your palate. I favour a sweet sauce; others might prefer one with a more cutting edge.

Wondered how fresh coriander leaf and dried coriander seeds come from the same plant? Try eating the green coriander seeds that appear once the plants have flowered.

sautéed carrots and courgettes with green coriander seeds

2 tablespoons olive oil | 15g butter | 225g carrots, peeled and halved lengthwise, and finely sliced | 1 garlic clove, peeled and crushed | 225g small, firm courgettes, ends removed and finely sliced | 1 teaspoon green coriander seeds, lightly crushed | sea salt and black pepper

serves 6

1 Heat the oil and butter in a frying pan and add the carrot. Fry over a low heat for about 5 minutes, or until it becomes slightly soft. Add the garlic and cook for a further 2 minutes. Add the courgette and cook for another 4–5 minutes, or until it, too, just wilts.

2 Stir in the crushed coriander seeds and season with salt and pepper. Fry over a high heat for a final minute, then serve at once.

These delicious potatoes are cooked until soft inside and golden and crusty outside.

rosemary roast potatoes

4 large main-crop potatoes, scrubbed and cut into cubes of about 2.5cm | 4 tablespoons olive oil | coarse sea salt and black pepper | 2–3 sprigs fresh rosemary

serves 6

1 Preheat the oven to 200°C/400°F/Gas mark 6.

2 Place the potato and oil in a large bowl, season well, then scrape the contents of the bowl into a roasting pan. Add the rosemary, and roast in the preheated oven for about 1 hour, turning from time to time.

I've made this cake with raspberries and with apple, but blackberries are special. Do use butter – there is never any need to eat cake, so when we do we should eat good cake.

warm blackberry and brown sugar cake

220g blackberries | 190g soft butter, plus extra for greasing | 190g plain flour | 2 teaspoons baking powder | 190g light muscovado sugar | 3 large eggs | I teaspoon vanilla extract
For the topping 55g butter | 55g light muscovado sugar | 85g shelled pecan nuts, chopped | I teaspoon freshly ground cinnamon

makes I cake

1   Preheat the oven to 180°C/350°F/Gas mark 4. Begin by mixing the topping ingredients together. Scatter half the blackberries over the base of a greased 20cm springform tin, then spoon the topping evenly over them.

2   To start the cake, sift the flour with the baking powder. Cream the butter with the sugar, beating in the egg and vanilla, then lightly folding in the flour and remaining blackberries. Spoon this over the topping and bake the cake in the preheated oven for 45–55 minutes, or until it starts to pull from the sides of the tin. Allow the cake to cool for 10 minutes before turning out on to a serving plate. Serve warm with crème fraîche ice-cream (see page 157).

Should late summer winds make a walk in the garden chilly, warm spiced juice helps.

warm spiced apple juice

I litre good apple juice | 7.5cm cinnamon stick | ½ nutmeg, crushed | 3–4 cloves, crushed | I apple, cored and thinly sliced into rings

makes I litre

1   Warm the juice with the spices, then turn off the heat and allow to infuse for 2–4 hours.

2   Reheat the juice before serving, strain into a jug and float in the apple rings.

Crème fraîche gives this ice-cream a sharp tang that perfectly complements the buttery cake above. Full-fat yoghurt works just as well as the crème fraîche.

crème fraîche ice-cream

4 large egg yolks | 110g caster sugar | 300ml double cream | 1 vanilla pod, roughly chopped | 225g full-fat crème fraîche

makes ¾ litre

1   Whisk the egg yolks with the sugar until light. Gently warm the cream with the vanilla pod until boiling point is reached. Remove the cream from the heat, and gradually whisk it and the vanilla into the egg mixture.

2   Now return the custard to the pan and, over a low heat and stirring constantly, cook the custard until it thickens. This will take about 5 minutes. Do not let the mixture boil. Tip the contents of the saucepan into a liquidiser and whizz on high speed for 30 seconds. Pass through a sieve to remove the vanilla pod. Whisk in the crème fraîche and allow the mixture to cool.

3   Freeze in an electric churn according to the manufacturer's instructions, or in the freezer in a shallow bowl. If you choose the freezer, you will need to beat the ice-cream two or three times as it freezes to break down the ice crystals. Remove the ice-cream from the freezer and place in the refrigerator for about 15 minutes before serving.

BASIC RECIPES

home-made shortcrust pastry

While it isn't always necessary to make pastry, it is simple to do, and you will have the taste of butter enhancing your dish.

110g cold butter | 170g plain flour | 1 large egg yolk | sea salt | about 2 tablespoons water

1 Cut the butter into small pieces. Sift the flour into a roomy bowl and rub in the butter until the texture is like crumbs. Add the egg yolk, a pinch of salt and enough very cold water to form a stiff dough. Mix well.

2 Chill for 30 minutes, wrapped in clingfilm, then roll out.

yeast-based sourdough starter

Sourdough starters were one of the first ways of making leavened bread. The idea is that a little of yesterday's loaf is added to today's. This starter, once set up, sits happily in the refrigerator. Use the starter in any recipe that calls for flour; add it to breakfast pancakes or scones for a lighter, tastier result.

First stage **1½ teaspoons dried yeast | 140g plain flour | 220ml warm water**

Second stage **140g plain flour | 220ml milk | 85g caster sugar**

1 Mix the first-stage ingredients in a glass, china or plastic bowl. Cover and leave in a warm place for three days, stirring daily. By this time the mixture should be frothy and have a sour smell.

2 Add the second-stage ingredients. Stir well – don't worry if the mixture looks a little lumpy – then cover and place in the refrigerator. Stir daily. After five days the starter is ready.

3 To keep this going, add 2 tablespoons each of flour and milk, and 1 teaspoon caster sugar, each time you take 4 tablespoons of starter out.

basic bread

This dough can be used for pizza bases, lardy cake, foccacia You are limited only by your imagination.

1 walnut-sized piece fresh yeast, or 1 scant tablespoon dried yeast | ½ teaspoon runny honey | 300ml hand-hot water | 500g strong white flour | 1 teaspoon fine sea salt | 4 tablespoons fruity olive oil

1 Cream the fresh yeast with the honey, add the water and mix. Sprinkle on a tablespoon of the flour and leave to stand for 15 minutes, or until frothy. For dried yeast, mix the honey into the water, then sprinkle on the yeast, stirring well, and continue as above.

2 Mix the salt into the flour, then add the yeast mixture and the olive oil. Work into a ball of dough, then turn on to a board and knead for 5–8 minutes. The texture will change and the dough will become smoother and elastic. Return to an oiled bowl, cover with a cloth and put in a warm spot to rise.

3 Once the dough has doubled in size (about 1 hour), knock it back and knead lightly. Now add your chosen seasonings or simply shape the dough and put on a baking sheet to prove. The dough will double in size more quickly this time, depending on room temperature, about 30 minutes.

4 Preheat the oven to 200°C/400°F/Gas mark 6 and when hot bake the bread for about 20–30 minutes, until golden brown and hollow if tapped on the base.

stock

Stock is one of the main building bricks of restaurant cooking. It's often said that home-made stock is the only stock anyone who cares about good food can tolerate, but we all use the ready made stuff from time to time. I have been known to use a bottle of stock concentrate when speed is of the essence. Often wine, apple juice or plain tap water works well, but if you're making risotto you must have good home-made stock. Remember, the stockpot is not a magic porridge pot and whatever you put in will come out, so no three-day-old roast chicken carcasses and tired vegetables. Only use fresh – i.e. uncooked bones and good-quality veg. Cut vegetables to a size that allows them to cook in the time the stock will boil. For example, fish stock cooks for 15–20 minutes, so bits of carrot, onion etc must be tiny. Beef stock that boils for 4 hours can have whole vegetables thrown in. Be wary of using too much celery, as the flavour quickly overpowers all others. Stock is never seasoned with salt, as stock is an ingredient.

fish stock

When choosing fish bones for a fish stock, turbot bones are the best, followed by other flat fish such as brill and sole. Bass bones can be used as well, as can hake, haddock and cod. But always white fish; never oily fish.

makes about 1 litre

30g butter or 2 tablespoons olive oil | 1 leek, cleaned and finely chopped | 1 onion, peeled and finely chopped | 1 rib celery, finely chopped | ½ fennel bulb, finely chopped | 1.5kg fish bones (see above) | 300ml dry white wine | 2 sprigs each parsley, thyme | 1 teaspoon white peppercorns | 1 unwaxed lemon (optional)

1 Melt the butter in a pan and gently fry the vegetables in this until they soften slightly.

2 Chop the fish bones roughly, then add to the pot. Sweat them for 2–3 minutes, then add the wine and just enough water to cover the bones. Put in the herbs and peppercorns. Bring to the boil rapidly, skimming off the grey scum that rises to the surface. Simmer for 20 minutes, then remove from the heat. If you have time, lay thin slices of lemon on the stock and leave for 30 minutes. This gives it a lovely lemon tang.

3 Allow the stock to cool for 30 minutes, then, without moving the pan, carefully ladle off the stock, leaving the debris in the pan. Fish stock should be used within two days.

vegetable stock

Use this stock for tasty vegetarian dishes, soups and risottos.
makes about 1 litre

**1–2 tablespoons light vegetable oil | 1 onion, peeled
and finely chopped | 2 leeks, cleaned and chopped |
1–2 garlic cloves, peeled and crushed | 4 ribs celery,
roughly chopped | 2 large carrots, scrubbed and cut
into chunks | 2 plum tomatoes, roughly chopped |
1 sprig each of thyme and parsley | 1 bay leaf |
8 black peppercorns**

1 Place all the ingredients in a large pan and cover with cold
water. Bring to the boil and simmer for 20 minutes.
2 Pour the stock into a glass bowl or jar, and leave to allow
the flavours to infuse. Before use, strain through a fine sieve.
Keep in the refrigerator for up to a week.

brown chicken stock

This is my favourite stock, and the one I find most useful.
Use fresh chicken carcasses or chicken wing tips to make it.
This method can be used to make beef stock using beef
bones and boiling for 4 hours.
makes 1.5 litres

**4–5 raw chicken carcasses | 4 tablespoons olive oil |
1 large sprig thyme | 3 large carrots, scrubbed |
3 onions, peeled | 2–3 ribs celery | 2 medium leeks,
well washed | a few black peppercorns | fresh parsley
or tarragon to finish**

1 Roughly chop the carcasses and place in a large roasting
pan. Drizzle with about half the olive oil, add a few sprigs of
the thyme and roast in a hot oven at 220°C/425°F/Gas
mark 7, turning the bones often, for 20–30 minutes.
2 Place the roughly chopped vegetables in a large stockpot
with the remaining olive oil, and cook over a moderate heat
until the vegetables soften and turn a rich golden brown.
3 Lift the chicken carcasses and add to the pot of
vegetables, along with the thyme and peppercorns. Pour on
just enough cold water to cover. Bring rapidly to the boil,
skimming off any scum, and simmer for 1 hour.
4 Line a kitchen sieve with damp muslin or a damp tea towel,
and strain the stock through this. Pour it into a suitable container,
add a bunch of fresh tarragon or parsley, and leave to infuse.
5 This stock should lightly gel when cold. It keeps for up to
seven days in the refrigerator if boiled vigorously every
second day. It freezes well.

white chicken stock

Omit the olive oil and the browning of the meat and
vegetables. Simply pile the ingredients into a stockpot, cover
with water and proceed as above.

CONVERSION CHARTS

weight

metric	imperial
5g	⅛oz
10g	¼oz
15g	½oz
25-30g	1oz
35g	1¼oz
40g	1½oz
50g	1¾oz
55g	2oz
60g	2¼oz
70g	2½oz
85g	3oz
90g	3¼oz
100g	3½oz
115g	4oz
125g	4½oz
140g	5oz
150g	5½oz
175g	6oz
200g	7oz
225g	8oz
250g	9oz
275g	9¾oz
280g	10oz
300g	10½oz
325g	11½oz
350g	12oz
375g	13oz
400g	14oz
425g	15oz
450g	1lb
500g	1lb 2oz
550g	1lb 4oz
600g	1lb 5oz
650g	1lb 7oz
700g	1lb 9oz
750g	1lb 10oz
800g	1lb 12oz
900g	2lb

volume

metric	imperial
15ml	½fl oz
30ml	1oz
50ml	2fl oz
75ml	2½fl oz
100ml	3½fl oz
125ml	4fl oz
150ml	5fl oz (¼ pint)
175ml	6fl oz
200ml	7fl oz
225ml	8fl oz
250ml	9fl oz
300ml	10fl oz (½ pint)
350ml	12fl oz
400ml	14fl oz
425ml	15fl oz (¾ pint)
450ml	16fl oz
500ml	18fl oz
600ml	20fl oz (1 pint)
700ml	1¼ pints
850ml	1½ pints
1 litre	1¾ pints
1.2 litres	2 pints

These charts are reproduced
with the kind permission of
The Guild of Food Writers

INDEX